VAN LIFE COOKBOOK

First published in the United Kingdom
in 2022 by
Pavilion
43 Great Ormond Street
London
WC1N 3HZ

ISBN 978-1-91168-218-9

A CIP catalogue record for this book is available from the British Library.
10 9 8 7 6 5 4 3 2 1

MIX
Paper from
responsible sources
FSC® C023419
FSC
www.fsc.org

Reproduction by Mission Productions, Hong Kong
Printed and bound in Italy by L.E.G.O. S.p.A.
www.pavilionbooks.com

Commissioning editors: Lucy Smith
and Cara Armstrong
Copyeditor: Anne Sheasby
Design manager: Nicky Collings
Photographer: Holly Farrier
Food Stylists: Becks Wilson and Danny Jack
Prop Styling: Rachel Vere and Joanna Resiak
Production manager: Phil Brown

Resourceful
recipes for life
on the road:
from small
spaces to the
great outdoors

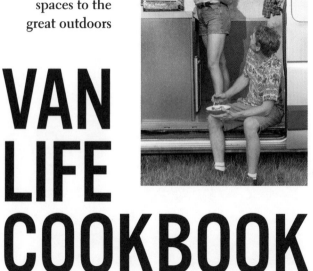

VAN LIFE COOKBOOK

DANNY JACK   HAILEE KUKURA

PAVILION

Introduction

Welcome to the *Van Life Cookbook*. This book is primarily a handy, visual guide packed full of tried and tested recipes that celebrate the unexpected joys and opportunities that modest spaces can bring to cooking – be it in a campervan or caravan, on a canal boat, at home, on a budget, or all of the above.

It aims to go beyond a collection of dishes that can be made on a two-ring gas stove or campfire. It's about a way of cooking and eating that saves time and money, is good for the belly and finds the best in your immediate environment. It encourages you to dig below the surface and look past the convenience of the supermarket, 'quick fixes' and the occasional disappointing restaurant or takeaway, and to discover a whole world of independent producers and hidden gems. From stumbling upon wild garlic growing abundantly in early spring to folk selling fresh, juicy cherries and strawberries in lay-bys in mid-summer; even free-range eggs can be found throughout much of the year at the end of someone's driveway.

Thrifty purchases, foraged finds and a collection of solid recipes will encourage cooks of all abilities and anyone with fire, a few pots and a knife to cook more creatively using what is close to hand. Maximizing time outdoors, minimizing time in supermarket queues and eating well is a win-win for everyone – and this kind of inventive preparation of food feeds creativity and nourishes a conscious approach in the kitchen. Most of all it's fun.

All the recipes are made from scratch, using mostly wholefoods and without any electrical equipment, so we hope to encourage readers to learn and cook more. Just a little bit of time, effort and appetite for this approach will be richly rewarded.

Some readers may not always feel adventurous in the way they prepare food, but almost everyone knows and values a good meal when they taste it. The recipes are designed for a limited set-up and budget – we've found that working within these constraints offers up creativity, builds autonomy and is just that little bit more rewarding. This extends to buying things second-hand, too, finding bargains like pots, pans and utensils at flea markets and charity shops along the way.

We've noticed a surge in people of all ages seeking alternative ways of living, being closer to nature and changing their lifestyle to become more self-sufficient. Written through the lens of our own travels, visiting friends, exploring the UK and travelling to the United States to visit family, we created this book for those hungry for that sense of freedom and adventure, seeking community and a deeper connection with food and where it comes from.

A further note: while many of the recipes in this book are vegetarian and/or plant-based/vegan, some do include meat, fish or shellfish. Our diet is 90 per cent vegetarian and that's reflected in this book. When we do eat meat, we try to source it directly from farm shops and choose high-welfare products or in-season game. When eating seafood, we try to buy from small day boats or reputable farms, avoiding any species on protected lists. We try to be discerning and maintain a level of scepticism; genuine transparency around accredited schemes, labelling and the like can be complicated but our only real advice is to just do your own research, trust your taste buds, and you're sure to be happy and feel good about what you're eating. There are no rules, only what feels right, and tasty, of course.

Tips, Tricks and Kitchen Hacks

When preparing food outdoors or in small spaces, having a few tips and tricks in your repertoire can help a lot. The right piece of equipment in the right place is essential; this mostly comes down to thoughtful use of storage and a well-organized, user-friendly kitchen. By streamlining your space, you can save time and energy, which frees up more time for kicking back. You can save on the washing up, too.

Handy Tips

- Place a tea towel or wet kitchen paper under the chopping board to stop it slipping.
- Use a tea towel as a drying rack, wringing it out between uses.
- Use the same size, dedicated containers for food prep and storage: 1 litre/1¾ pints is ideal.
- If you don't have lids, use plates or large bowls to make water boil faster, save on fuel and help keep food warm.
- Use old food containers to hold vegetable scraps while prepping.
- A washing-up bowl saves water and time.
- A magnetic knife rack is relatively cheap and a great way of freeing up space in the kitchen. It also keeps your knives in good shape.
- Jam jars. Screw the lid underneath a shelf and you have a cheap, effective storage solution.
- A small cafetière or robust teapot – loose leaf tea is often nicer, reduces plastic waste and saves money in the long run.
- Use catering crates or boxes that stack to help you store other van items. You can sometimes find them being thrown out from restaurants or bakeries.
- Invest in a good thermos. A double-walled reusable water bottle to carry both hot and cold drinks works well, too.
- Make sure you have a good cooler if you don't have a refrigerator.
- A lightweight, folding four-person table for al fresco dining.
- Foraging tools: guide books/basket/laundry bag/pocket knife/trowel/reusable ziplock bags for foraged food.

Our Recommended Lists

Initially we were reluctant to provide a long list of essential equipment and ingredients required to cook the recipes in this book. This can sometimes feel like a barrier to getting started; however, all of the below storecupboard staples feature multiple times in our recipes and are genuinely versatile ingredients that will likely become your favourites, too. In addition, many of our recipes feature options and substitutions so that you can use what you have immediately available or is in season.

Ingredients

- In our recipes, we use fine sea salt for general seasoning during cooking and flaked sea salt for finishing and garnishing dishes
- Black peppercorns (freshly ground with a good grinder)
- Smoked paprika
- Coriander seeds
- Fennel seeds
- Ground cumin
- Ground turmeric
- Fish sauce, or you can substitute with lime juice and salt as a vegan option
- Dried chilli flakes
- Hot chilli sauce (to make your own Fermented Chilli Sauce, see page 133)
- Canned anchovies
- We tend to use dark soy sauce or tamari in our recipes (note tamari is gluten-free)
- Extra virgin olive oil and regular olive oil. All our recipes simply refer to olive oil in the ingredients lists – in all these instances, we recommend that you use extra virgin olive oil
- Coconut oil
- Sesame oil
- Cider vinegar
- Date syrup
- Nutritional yeast

Cooking Equipment

Our recipes have been designed for a minimal set-up. This means cooking on two gas rings or over an open fire (or BBQ), with conservative use of gas and water. The majority of recipes in this book will only ever call for two pans at a time, and while none of the methods require the use of an oven or electrical equipment, some elements may be made easier with the use of a blender or electric hand whisk. If you have access to these gadgets, use your judgement with recipes. As a minimum, we do recommend the following for your kitchen set-up.

- Chopping boards: One large and one small, in case two people want to prep at the same time.
- Sharp kitchen knives: Ideally kept on a magnetic rack to save from blunting.
- Frying pans: A large, non-stick frying pan is a must. Ideally, a cast iron skillet, too, which can be used on an open fire and will last a lifetime if you season regularly and look after it.
- Saucepans and pots: Two pots are adequate. Have one large pot for soups, stews, curries and boiling pasta and large grains, and one smaller saucepan for eggs, sauces, porridge, rice, grains and desserts. With lids preferably, although you can always use a plate in its place. A third medium-sized pot could be useful, but only if you have the space.
- Mixing bowls: Stainless steel, stackable ones are ideal. One large and one small for tossing and serving salads, whipping cream and making dressings and sauces.
- Utensils: Our essentials include a whisk, spatula, wooden spoons, can opener, corkscrew, cutlery, metal tongs and a small, flat cheese grater with a handle. Microplanes are pretty handy for fresh ginger, garlic and fresh Parmesan.
- Colander: Useful but we often do without by carefully straining with a plate held over the pot, allowing the cooking liquid but not the ingredients to escape.

- Scales or cup measures: We're aware that carrying digital scales may not be a priority but they will be the most efficient way of following the recipes. You can buy small scales online fairly cheaply and they won't take up much space. Alternatively cup measurements are a good metric and can be used with the following conversions:
  1 cup = 16 tbsp or 240ml/8½fl oz
  ½ cup = 8 tbsp or 120ml/4fl oz
  1 tbsp = 15ml/approx. 15g/½oz
  1 tsp = 5ml/approx. 5g/⅛oz
- Glass or plastic containers with lids and jam jars: The award for the most disorderly area of a kitchen goes to the container department. Having lots of stackable containers all the same size with lids will help keep your food more organized, stay fresher for longer, keep you sane and take up less room. Containers can also double up as sandwich boxes or help you organize prep when cooking. BPA food-safe plastic, glass or stainless steel with wax seal lids are the best options here. You could even go so far as to measure the shelves in your refrigerator or cooler and buy containers that fit those dimensions.
- A stack of clean tea towels: Multiple absorbent tea towels are a lifesaver. Rotate as needed so wet tea towels can dry. Reusable/washable kitchen cloths offer a good alternative to disposables.
- Disinfectant/cleaner: In the van and at home we use a 1:3 ratio of spirit vinegar to water in a reusable spray bottle, plus a few drops of essential oil or lemon to make it smell nice.
- Kitchen paper: Kitchen paper/roll can be super helpful but also wasteful. We buy the large catering 'blue rolls' from pound shops as opposed to standard kitchen paper, but try to avoid using it at all if possible and instead use reusable absorbent kitchen cloths or tea towels (see above).

Cooking Tips: The Basics

Follow the cooking tips below for faultless staples every time. You'll save effort and avoid any mushiness, unnecessary draining or excess waste.

Rice: All you need to achieve lovely, fluffy rice is a ratio of 2:1 water to rice at the start. This simple method works every time for most varieties. Measure your desired quantity of rice into a cup and pour into a saucepan (you can rinse your rice first, if you like, but it's not necessary). Next, pour cold water into the same cup, to the same level as the rice, and pour it into the saucepan, then repeat so you have double the volume of water to rice. Put over a high heat with a big pinch of salt and bring to the boil, then reduce the heat to a low simmer and cover with a lid or plate. Once covered, the cooking time should take about 7–10 minutes for white rice, 15–20 minutes for brown. Once the water is fully absorbed, remove from the heat, then keep the cooked rice covered to rest for a few minutes or until you are ready to dish up.

Pasta: Generously salt the cooking water – there is a saying that goes it should be as salty as the Mediterranean Sea. Add a splash of olive oil and then add the pasta to the boiling water. Always save some of the cooking water to use in your pasta sauce for the perfect consistency. The cooking time for dried pasta is usually around 10–12 minutes. All weights and cooking times given for pasta in our recipes are for dried (not fresh) pasta.

Noodles (rice, egg or wheat): Some noodles only require soaking in boiling water for 10 minutes or longer, but others require boiling for 1–2 minutes. Once drained, mix with a little neutral or sesame oil to stop them sticking together until needed for the dish. Always check the instructions on the packet for best results.

Potatoes: New potatoes can be left whole (or halved, if large), and regular, larger potatoes are best cut into quarters or equal-sized pieces. Add to a pot of cold water, season generously with salt, then bring to the boil and cook until just tender. Drain in a colander and eat straight away, or cool down for potato salad or fried potatoes below.

For fried potatoes, cut into the desired shape once cool enough to handle. Heat about 2 tablespoons of neutral or olive oil in a large, non-stick frying pan, add the potato and cook over a high heat, turning once, until coloured and crispy on both sides, about 5–7 minutes. Season with salt in the pan, then serve (before serving, you can drain them on kitchen paper or a clean tea towel to remove some of the oil after cooking).

Quinoa: Follow a similar method to the rice by adding double the amount of water to the grain with a pinch of salt, then bring to the boil and simmer, covered, for 10–12 minutes. Turn off the heat and leave to rest for at least 5 minutes, then fluff with a fork.

Puy lentils: Use a 1:3 ratio of dried (rinsed) lentils to water (so 100g/3½oz of lentils to 300ml/10fl oz of water) and follow the same method for the quinoa above. For larger grains, such as pearl barley and spelt, boil in a generous amount of water until soft, usually around 20–30 minutes, then drain. Season once cooked.

For leafy greens: We often find steam-frying is quicker and more energy efficient. Simply heat your large, non-stick frying pan until very hot, add the prepared greens (we like to use kale, spinach, chard, etc.), a tablespoon of oil (we like coconut oil for greens, but olive oil also works), a little salt and a splash of water, then put a lid on and cook over a high heat for about 1 minute until wilted, tender and vibrant green.

Cooking with Fire

It takes about 30–45 minutes for a BBQ to reach cooking temperature using wood or charcoal (sizes vary, of course). The guide below should help:

- Still black or grey with flames: not ready yet.
- Glowing white hot with red centres: almost ready; wait a little longer.
- Ashy white and grey but still very hot: ready for cooking.
- If you are cooking over an open fire, as with a charcoal BBQ, wait until the embers are ready before starting to cook over them using a grill/rack.

BREAKFAST *and* BRUNCH

Brown rice oatmeal with ginger and honey

A good alternative to regular porridge, this is our sweeter take on congee – a simple, popular Chinese porridge dish and excellent if you're feeling under the weather. It's also a great use of leftover rice. The grated ginger is particularly soothing if you have indigestion and need something easy on the stomach; here, it is gently infused with milk to impart a subtle warmth throughout the dish. Best finished with a drizzle of good-quality honey.

Serves 2

For the brown rice oatmeal
350ml/12fl oz milk (dairy or plant-based) or a mix of milk and water
a small piece of fresh ginger, peeled and grated
1 tsp ground cinnamon
250g/9oz cooked short-grain brown rice (leftover is best)
1 tsp soft light brown sugar or caster sugar
a pinch of salt

For the topping
2 tbsp honey, date syrup or other sweetener
1 banana, thinly sliced (optional)
a handful of chopped raw nuts of your choice (optional)

Simply put your milk of choice (or milk and water) in a saucepan with the ginger and cinnamon and bring to a gentle simmer for a few minutes.

Add in your cooked rice, stirring well to get rid of the lumps. Stir in the sugar and pinch of salt.

Cook for 7–8 minutes until fully heated through and to your desired consistency. If it's too thick, add a splash more milk and cook for a minute longer.

Spoon the oatmeal into two bowls. Drizzle with your sweetener and top with the sliced banana and chopped nuts (if using). Serve.

Buckwheat shortstack

Pancakes served American-style. Known as 'shortstacks', they are quite a bit thicker than the crêpes you find in Europe and nicely soak up the syrup and juice from the berries. If you prefer the thinner variety, just add a bit more milk to your batter.

Serves 2–3 (makes about 6 large pancakes)

For the batter

150g/5½oz buckwheat flour or 150g/5½oz plain wholemeal flour
2 tsp golden caster sugar or white caster sugar
1 tsp baking powder
1 small pear or apple, cored and grated (optional)
250ml/9fl oz milk (dairy or plant-based), at room temperature
2 eggs, separated
about 1 tbsp butter, for frying

To serve

1 tbsp date syrup, honey, maple syrup or sweetener of your choice
2–3 tbsp Greek-style yogurt (dairy or plant-based)
1 x 150g/5½oz punnet of berries, such as blueberries or raspberries

For the batter, mix the flour, sugar, baking powder, grated pear or apple (if using), milk and egg yolks in a mixing bowl with a whisk until smooth.

In a separate bowl, whisk the egg whites until soft peaks form, then fold into the flour mix. Cover and rest for at least 10 minutes.

Heat your large, non-stick frying pan over a medium-high heat and grease generously with some of the butter. Ladle some batter into the centre of the pan and leave to cook, then flip when the batter begins to bubble in the middle, about 2 minutes. Cook on the second side for 1–2 minutes, until the pancake is light brown on both sides and a little crispy on the edges. Remove to a plate and keep warm.

Repeat the process, re-greasing the pan with butter as needed and cooking one pancake at a time, keeping the cooked pancakes covered with a clean tea towel until all the pancakes are cooked.

Divide them up between your plates, drizzling your sweetener over the top. Serve each portion with a dollop of yogurt and a scattering of berries on top.

Mum's porridge with hazelnuts and maple syrup

There's a world porridge-making competition held each year at Carrbridge Village Hall in the Cairngorms, Scotland. The first prize is a golden spurtle, a wooden utensil for stirring porridge to perfection. Competitors can only use water, oats and salt. It's all in the method. My mum and dad are originally from Stirlingshire and Fife, they raised our family in Wales, and then returned to their roots a few years ago. They have since perfected their porridge recipe. Note: the end of a wooden spoon works just as well here.

Serves 2

135g/4¾oz porridge oats
340ml/11¾fl oz milk (or cold water, if you prefer the traditional method)
a pinch of salt, plus extra (optional) to serve

To serve (all optional)
50g/1¾oz chopped raw hazelnuts or other chopped raw nuts of your choice
100g/3½oz chopped fresh fruit, such as apple or pear
2 tbsp maple syrup or other sweetener
2 tbsp milk or double cream

Place the oats, 250ml/9fl oz of cold water, the milk (or extra water) and pinch of salt into a saucepan over a medium heat. Using a wooden spoon or spurtle, stir the mixture to distribute the ingredients evenly.

Heat slowly, stirring gently and consistently to prevent the mixture sticking to the bottom of the pan. After about 4 minutes, the mixture should come to a gentle boil with bursting, popping bubbles that release steam.

Reduce the heat further and keep stirring for another 3–4 minutes. Don't let it catch on the bottom.

When it's ready, the porridge should stick to the wooden spoon and have a dropping consistency. If it's too thick, a little extra water (or milk) can be stirred in to loosen it.

Serve up into bowls and sprinkle with a little salt for the traditional method. Alternatively, prepare your toppings, scattering and pouring over the top as desired. Enjoy with a big spoon.

Pyttipanna potatoes

Pyttipanna is a Swedish breakfast hash usually made with leftover cooked pork and potatoes. It translates as 'small pieces in a pan'. In my early twenties, I lived near the IKEA in Bristol and briefly got hooked on their frozen version. This home-made version is vegetarian and made with fresh ingredients for an equally tasty, wholesome start to the day.

Serves 2

300g/10½oz potatoes (waxy varieties are best), washed with skin on and cut into 1cm/½ inch cubes
olive oil, for frying
1 small onion, finely diced
2 garlic cloves, crushed
150g/5½oz mushrooms, diced
1 small carrot, washed and diced or grated
100g/3½oz leftover cooked vegetables, such as broccoli or courgettes, root vegetables, tomatoes, spinach or peppers, finely chopped (optional)
50g/1¾oz vegetarian (or vegan) cheese (such as mature Cheddar, Parmesan-style or feta), crumbled or grated (optional)
a few sprigs of parsley, dill or chives, chopped
salt and freshly ground black pepper

To serve
2 eggs, or Tofu Scramble (see page 85) for a plant-based version
hot chilli sauce, Harissa Sauce (see page 135) or HP brown sauce or A1 steak sauce

Fry the potatoes in a little olive oil with a pinch of salt in a large, non-stick frying pan over a low-medium heat for 15–20 minutes until soft. Drain and set aside in a large bowl to keep warm.

Next, and in the same pan, add the onion and garlic with a little more olive oil and another pinch of salt. Cook for 2 minutes, then add the mushrooms and carrot and cook for a further 5 minutes.

Add your potatoes and mix together, seasoning to taste with salt and pepper.

If desired, add the leftover cooked vegetables and fry for another minute. The pan will be quite full but keep mixing until everything is combined. Finish with the cheese (if using) and fresh herbs, then transfer to the large bowl, cover and set aside.

Using the same frying pan (wipe it clean first), turn up the heat, add a little more olive oil and fry your eggs until cooked to your liking (a runny yolk is best). Alternatively, you can make some tofu scramble (see page 85).

To serve, divide the potato hash between plates. Place a fried egg or some tofu scramble on top of the hash and then top with chilli, harissa or brown sauce. If you have some, pickles (such as pickled beetroot or pickled red onions) on the side are traditional in Sweden.

Black pudding hash with fried duck egg

This was a lunch special at a well-known Edinburgh restaurant called The Dogs, where I worked from 2009–10 and where Hailee and I first met.

Serves 4

500g/1lb 2oz potatoes, peeled and quartered (choose a floury variety, such as Maris Piper or King Edward)
200g/7oz black pudding
2 tbsp HP brown sauce or A1 steak sauce, plus extra to serve
1 tbsp neutral or olive oil, plus a little extra (or butter), for frying the eggs
4 duck eggs (or hen eggs, if you prefer)
salt and freshly ground black pepper

Add the potatoes to a pot of salted cold water, bring to the boil and cook until tender, then drain (keep the hot water for later if you prefer boiled or poached eggs). Set the potatoes aside until cool enough to handle.

Using your hands, break up the potatoes in a bowl and then crumble in the black pudding. Add in the brown or steak sauce and some salt and pepper, mixing everything together with your hands until fully combined.

Shape the mixture into 4 equal-sized burger patties and squish down a little. They can be cooked right away, but it's best if they are chilled in the refrigerator for an hour first.

When you are ready to cook, get a large, non-stick frying pan and bring it to a medium heat. Add the oil and gently fry the patties over a medium-low heat for 15–20 minutes, until crispy on the outside and cooked throughout, carefully turning them over halfway through to make sure they don't burn. You could put a lid or plate over the pan to help steam-fry a little.

To serve, transfer the patties to your plates, keeping them warm by covering. Using your pan again, turn up the heat and fry the eggs to your liking in a little extra oil (or melted butter), or poach or boil them in the reserved pot of hot water. A runny yolk is best.

Place each egg on top of the hash, with a dollop of brown or steak sauce to the side.

The
ORIGINAL
HP
SAUCE

Buckwheat tahini porridge

Our friend Ro made this buckwheat porridge recipe at a friend's birthday weekend and we became obsessed with the texture, nuttiness and ritual around making the cooked kernels, also known as 'kasha' in Eastern Europe. Looking to perfect our method, we ended up down a rabbit hole of peculiar techniques, such as resting the cooked kasha under a thick blanket for an hour. We didn't actually try this, but we found that covering for 5 minutes after cooking achieves that desired fluffy texture. If you decide to adjust your buckwheat quantities, it's a 2:1 ratio of water to buckwheat.

Serves 2

150g/5½ oz dried buckwheat groats
a pinch of salt
2–4 tbsp tahini
6 tbsp Greek-style yogurt (dairy or plant-based)
2–4 tbsp date syrup or sweetener of your choice
1 banana, sliced (optional)

Pour 300ml/10fl oz of water into a pan and bring to a rolling boil.

While your water is coming to the boil, dry-toast the buckwheat in a hot, non-stick frying pan, moving it around until caramel brown and fragrant, about 3½ minutes.

Slowly add your toasted buckwheat to the boiling water with a pinch of salt. Reduce to a simmer and cook, covered with a lid or plate, for 8 minutes or until almost all the water has been absorbed.

Once finished, turn the heat off and leave to sit, covered with a lid and a clean tea towel on top, for at least 5 minutes.

Fluff up the buckwheat with a fork and divide between your bowls. Drizzle the tahini, yogurt and date syrup or sweetener over the top. Serve with sliced banana, if using.

Fruit and nut no-bake breakfast bars

A super quick, healthy breakfast or energy bar/ball that doesn't require any kit to make. The dates both sweeten and bind the ingredients together, and contrast nicely with the toasted oats. Good sustenance for those who don't eat much before midday. Make in advance and freeze, if they last that long!

Makes 10 bars or balls

300g/10½ oz stoned fresh dates (the softer the better – we like medjool), roughly chopped
150g/5½ oz raw cashew nuts, finely chopped
50g/1¾ oz raw almonds, finely chopped (or use an extra 50g/1¾ oz raw cashew nuts)
50g/1¾ oz porridge oats or dried coconut flakes (or a mixture), toasted

Prepare your dates and nuts first.

Next, place your non-stick frying pan on the stove and turn up the heat to medium-high. Toast the oats and/or coconut flakes until they start to brown and smell toasted, about 1–2 minutes.

Tip into a mixing bowl, cool slightly, then add the dates and nuts and mix together thoroughly with clean hands.

Use your hands to divide and shape the mix into 10 round balls, then keep in an airtight container in the refrigerator. Alternatively, press the mixture evenly over the base of a flat/shallow container (such as a square/rectangular plastic food box), then chill overnight in the refrigerator. Slice into rectangles or squares in the morning.

These will keep in an airtight container in the refrigerator for about a month. Alternatively, freeze them for up to 3 months. They thaw very quickly, so can be eaten almost straight out of the freezer.

French toast with walnuts and cream

A celebratory and indulgent start to the day. This recipe has birthday breakfast written all over it, but it's also perfect for using up any leftover bread. A great example of luxury and thrift working together seamlessly. You can use maple syrup or honey for a more traditional version if you can't find any elderflowers in season.

Serves 4 (2 slices each)

100ml/3½fl oz milk (dairy or plant-based)
5 eggs
a pinch of ground cinnamon
1 tsp caster sugar
1 tsp vanilla extract (optional)
8 slices of bread (brioche is traditional, but any bread of your choice will work)
1–2 tbsp butter, for frying

To serve
75g/2¾oz walnuts, roughly chopped
3 tbsp Elderflower Cordial (see page 148) or sweetener of your choice, such as honey or maple syrup
4 dollops of double cream, crème fraîche or coconut cream

Toast the walnuts (for serving) in a large, dry, non-stick frying pan over a medium heat for about 1–2 minutes, then tip on to a plate and set aside. Keep the pan for frying the toast.

Next, whisk together the milk, eggs, cinnamon, sugar and vanilla in a mixing bowl.

Lightly pierce the tops of the bread slices with a fork. This makes the egg soak into the bread even more. Dip each slice of bread in the egg mix for 10 seconds or so on each side until each piece has soaked some of it up.

Melt a little butter in your frying pan until foaming and fry the eggy bread (two slices at a time) over a medium heat for 1–3 minutes on each side, until it has a nice golden brown colour and is firm. This means the egg is cooked. Remove to a plate and keep warm (or serve each batch as it's ready). Repeat the process until all the slices are cooked.

Plate up and drizzle over the elderflower cordial (if using) or sweetener of your choice, scatter with the toasted walnuts, then add your choice of cream in an artful dollop on each serving. Enjoy.

Overnight oats

This simple, easy-to-pack breakfast is similar to bircher muesli, which is basically grated apple, oats and milk combined and soaked overnight. We've experimented with quite a few versions and have found that dried mulberries are a winning ingredient. A perfectly formed dried fruit, they soak up the milk beautifully and are packed with vitamin C, too. The yogurt, if you have it, adds a lovely silkiness.

Makes 2 jam jarfuls

150g/5½oz porridge oats
3 tbsp raw almonds or other raw nuts, whole or roughly chopped
3 tbsp dried mulberries or stoned, chopped dates or raisins as an alternative
300ml/10fl oz milk (plant-based or dairy)
2 tbsp natural yogurt (plant-based or dairy, optional)
1 tbsp date syrup or other sweetener (optional)

Before you go to bed, prepare the recipe by dividing the ingredients evenly between two clean jam jars, then secure the lids tightly and shake well.

Refrigerate overnight and enjoy for breakfast the next morning.

If you prefer your oats slightly runnier, adjust the mixture accordingly by adding an extra splash of milk just before serving (then remember to make this same adjustment to begin with, next time you make this recipe).

Huevos 'Van'cheros

Huevos rancheros (or ranch-style eggs as they are known throughout Mexico and the US Southwest) was one of the first meals Hailee made for me and I've been in love ever since. This is our shared method for the road, using scrambled instead of fried eggs. The Pico de Gallo (see page 50) is optional here; store-bought salsa will work just as well instead. Just make sure you don't forget the hot sauce.

Serves 4

200g/7oz raw rice (any type)

For the beans

½ red onion, diced
4 garlic cloves, sliced
1 tbsp olive oil
½ small bunch of coriander, stalks finely diced, leaves saved for garnish
1 tomato, chopped
2 tbsp ground cumin
2 x 400g/14oz cans black beans, drained and rinsed
salt and freshly ground black pepper

For the rest

4 large corn tortillas (1 per person)
a knob of butter
8 eggs, whisked together with a fork and a little salt
200g/7oz mature Cheddar cheese, grated
Pico de Gallo (see page 50) or store-bought salsa, to taste
1 lime, cut into quarters
Tabasco sauce or similar hot sauce, to taste
4 dollops of soured cream or Greek-style yogurt (optional)

The first step is to make the rice – see page 12. Once cooked, keep it warm in the pan.

While your rice is simmering, take out a second pot for the beans. Cook the onion and garlic with a pinch of salt in the olive oil over a medium heat until translucent, about 5 minutes.

Add in the coriander stalks and chopped tomato. Cook for another minute, then add in the cumin and a splash of water and keep stirring for 5 minutes or so.

Add in your black beans, then add about a canful of water to cover them. Bring to the boil, then simmer over a medium heat for 20 minutes until the sauce is reduced and thickened, stirring occasionally. To finish, mash the beans a little with a fork and season to taste with salt and pepper. Reduce a little more, if they're too runny.

Recipe continued from p.30

Prepare the rest of your ingredients while the beans are cooking and rice is resting.

Take a large, dry, non-stick frying pan and heat until hot. Cook your tortillas, one at a time, over a high heat for about 30 seconds on each side, flipping them over once. Transfer to a plate and cover with a clean tea towel to keep warm. Repeat until they're all cooked.

Finally, make your scrambled eggs. In the tortilla pan, add in a knob of butter and your eggs. Keep over a low heat, stirring with a spatula and cooking through until the egg comes together with large folds but is still a little runny. Turn the heat off to finish cooking and keep warm.

Now to assemble. Place each tortilla flat on a plate and top with the rice, beans and some scrambled eggs. Sprinkle over the grated cheese, then top with the salsa. Garnish each portion with a wedge of lime, the coriander leaves and some hot sauce. Add a dollop of soured cream or yogurt to the side.

Menemen: Turkish one-pan eggs

A well-known Turkish breakfast dish. I'd always get this from a favourite breakfast spot in Stoke Newington, North London, called Cafe Z Bar. This area of the city has a large Turkish community and incredible restaurants as a result. This dish was always consistent and offered the perfect hangover cure – an unchallenging, delicious plate of spicy eggs with tomatoes and soft bread that could be eaten with a spoon. Cafe Z even served draught beer, which was sometimes needed.

Serves 2

1 red onion, finely sliced
2 garlic cloves, roughly chopped
1 fresh red chilli, roughly chopped, or 1 tsp chilli flakes, plus extra (optional) to serve
2 tbsp olive oil
1 small green pepper, deseeded and sliced
1 small red pepper, deseeded and sliced
2 tbsp smoked paprika (optional)
1 x 400g/14oz can tomatoes or 400g/14oz chopped fresh tomatoes
4–6 eggs
5 sprigs of parsley, leaves picked and roughly chopped
salt and freshly ground black pepper

To serve
olive oil, for drizzling
2–4 pitta bread or slices of soft white bread (1–2 per person)

In a large, non-stick frying pan, fry the onion, garlic and chilli or chilli flakes in the olive oil with a big pinch of salt over a medium heat for 5 minutes, stirring occasionally. Add the peppers and another pinch of salt and cook for a further 7 minutes.

Add the smoked paprika (if using) and stir together with the pepper and onion mix, then add the tomatoes. Swill about 100ml/3½fl oz of water around the empty tomato can, then pour into the pot. Bring to the boil, then simmer and reduce for 10 minutes, stirring occasionally.

You can make this mix ahead of time. Simply cool and store in an airtight container in the refrigerator for up to 2–3 days, then finish it later by going to the next step and reheating it before you add the eggs.

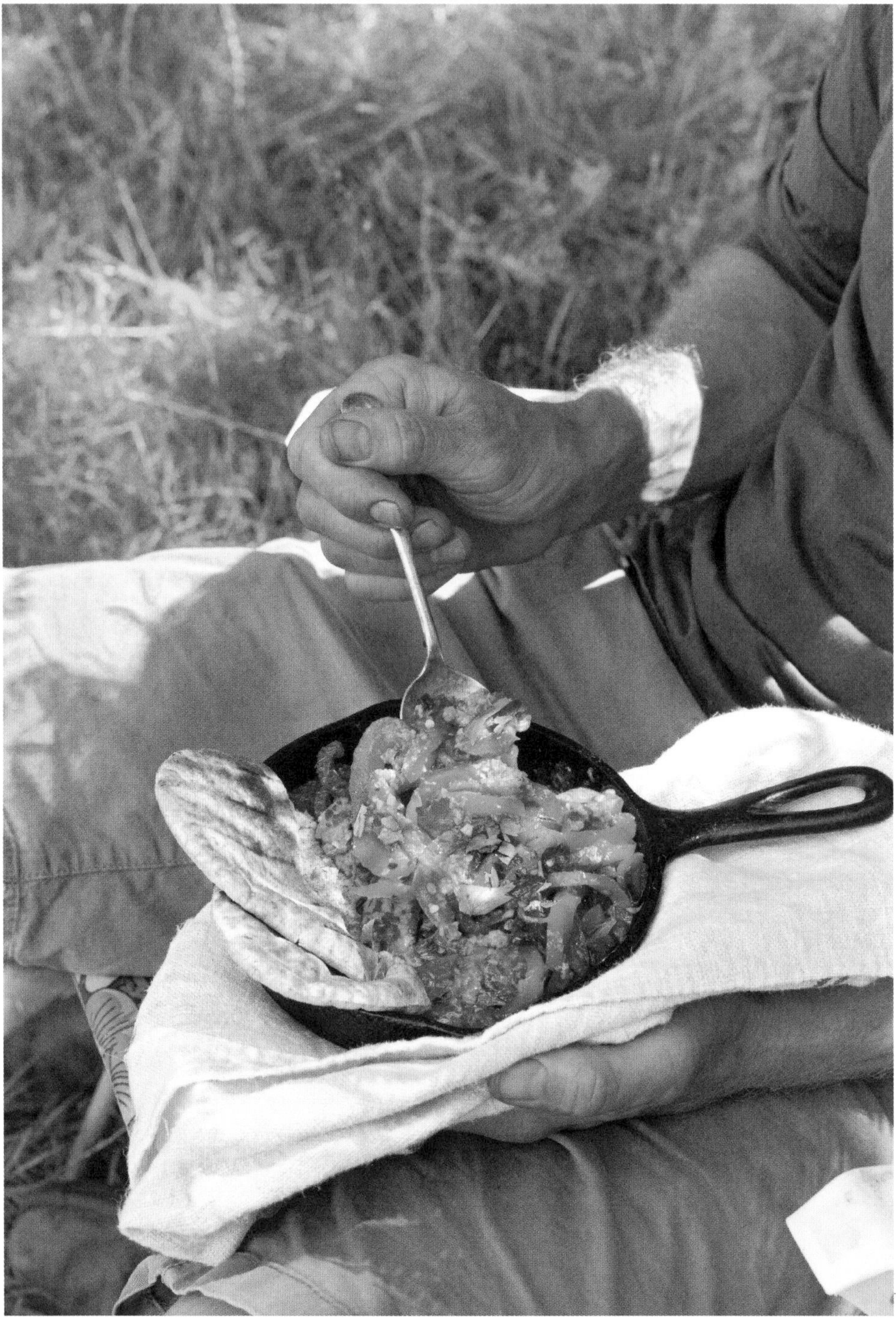

Recipe continued from p.33

Finish the dish by whisking up your eggs in a bowl and seasoning with salt and pepper. Make some space in your pan by scraping the pepper mixture to one side, away from the heat, and add the eggs to scramble on the other side.

Return to a low heat and, once almost scrambled, fold the eggs through the pepper mix, until fully combined, adding in the chopped parsley and more seasoning, if required. Turn off the heat, allowing the residual heat to cook the eggs a little more.

Divide between two plates, adding more chilli/chilli flakes, if desired, a drizzle of olive oil and some pitta bread (quickly warmed through in a non-stick frying pan, if you like) or soft bread to mop up the sauce.

Harissa beans on sourdough toast with poached egg and feta

Harissa beans are our go-to breakfast accompaniment. The base is essentially harissa spices cooked with onion and garlic, slowly stewed down with canned beans and tomatoes. The mix of saucy, spicy beans with a soft poached egg, sharp feta, and crunchy sprouts or rocket and the dukkah is a lovely combination (and hearty, too). Enjoy on thickly sliced sourdough.

Serves 4

For the harissa beans

3 garlic cloves, crushed
1 small fresh red chilli, deseeded and finely chopped
3 tbsp olive oil
1 red onion, finely diced
1 tsp ground cumin
1 tbsp smoked paprika
2 x 400g/14oz cans cannellini beans, drained and rinsed
1 x 400g/14oz can tomatoes
salt and freshly ground black pepper

To serve

1 tbsp Pumpkin Seed Dukkah (see page 131 – optional) or 1 tsp combined flaked sea salt and black pepper
4 eggs
4 thick slices of sourdough bread
75g/2¾oz feta cheese, crumbled
a large handful of alfalfa sprouts or rocket leaves (about 100g/3½oz)
olive oil, for drizzling

For the harissa beans, take a large pot and sweat down the garlic and chilli in the olive oil with a pinch of salt over a medium heat for 1 minute. Add your onion and continue to cook, stirring occasionally, for 10 minutes.

Next, stir in the cumin and paprika, then pour in the drained beans and the tomatoes, swilling some water in the tomato can (about a third of a canful) and adding that to the pot, too. Bring to the boil, then reduce the heat to a simmer, cover with a lid or plate and cook for 20 minutes, stirring occasionally. Season to taste with salt and pepper and keep warm until ready to serve.

Put a separate pot of water on to boil for the eggs, adding a little salt and the vinegar to help keep them together while cooking. Crack one of the eggs into the gently simmering water, making sure it's simmering again before adding the next. After 3–4 minutes, lift out each of your eggs with a large spoon. They'll be done when the white is opaque and there's a firm bounce on the yolk. Remove with a slotted spoon and put on a plate.

If you want your sourdough toasted, place in a large, dry, non-stick frying pan over a high heat for about 2 minutes or until browned on each side. Spoon the beans over the toast and place a poached egg on top of each portion. Finish with crumbled feta, sprouts or rocket, a drizzle of olive oil and a sprinkle of Dukkah (see page 131) and season to taste.

Wild mushrooms on toast

When I think of the best way to cook mushrooms, I always visualize them being done this way, especially if you've found them yourself after a successful day of foraging. It's even more ideal if you have a cast iron skillet to hand and a hot fire. The garlic butter keeps it classic and a little luxurious. Deglaze with a good-quality vinegar and serve on thickly sliced toast for a supremely satisfying brunch. Also works well with a poached egg on top, if desired.

Serves 2

600g/1lb 5oz mixed mushrooms (wild ones, if you're lucky), thickly sliced to finger width
40g/1½oz or 2 tbsp butter or olive oil
6 garlic cloves, crushed with a knife and roughly chopped
2 tbsp good-quality vinegar (ideally sherry, balsamic, red wine or aged malt vinegar)
2 eggs (optional)
2 thick slices of bread of your choice
salt and freshly ground black pepper

To garnish
a handful of rocket or chopped parsley
freshly grated Parmesan cheese, for sprinkling (optional)

Get a large, non-stick frying pan and add all the mushrooms to the pan with a large pinch of salt. Don't add anything else, it's not needed yet.

Cook over a medium-high heat for 5 minutes until some liquid starts to come out of the mushrooms.

Turn the heat down and push the mushrooms to one side. Add the butter or olive oil and the crushed garlic. Let the garlic cook for a minute before mixing it together with the mushrooms. It's okay if some mushrooms creep into the garlic when frying.

Once cooked and all the mushrooms are coated in the butter, deglaze the hot pan with the vinegar, turn off the heat and season to taste with salt and pepper. Set aside in a heatproof dish, cover with a lid and keep warm. Wipe your pan clean.

Poach or fry your eggs, if using, according to the recipes on pages 36 and 22 and make your toast (in a dry, non-stick frying pan over a high heat, if you don't have a toaster).

To serve, spoon the mushrooms over the toast with all the pan juices. Top with the eggs or leave plain. Garnish with some rocket or chopped parsley and a sprinkling of Parmesan, if you like.

LUNCH *and* SNACKS

Chunky tomato soup with cheddar and pickle sandwich

Who doesn't love tomato soup with a cheese sandwich? The soup here is essentially a recipe for a classic, home-made tomato sauce that you could use for a pasta dish (simply reduce the quantity of stock/water for a tomato ragù-type sauce). Cheese and Branston pickle is one of my favourite sandwiches, but you could use any chutney or relish for a winning combination. The creaminess of the cheese cuts through the sharp tomato for a warming, satisfying lunch every time.

Serves 4

For the tomato soup

3 tbsp olive oil
5 garlic cloves, crushed
4 sprigs of thyme, leaves picked
1 red or brown onion, diced
2 celery sticks, diced
1 carrot, washed and grated or diced
2 x 400g/14oz cans tomatoes
500ml/18fl oz vegetable stock or water
Handful of fresh basil leaves, torn or chopped (optional)
salt and freshly ground black pepper

For the sandwiches

4 tbsp butter, softened
8 slices of bread (any bread will do; sourdough is our favourite)
about 8 thick slices of extra mature Cheddar cheese
about 8 tbsp Branston pickle (kimchi or relish of your choice are good alternatives, too)

For the soup, simply pour the olive oil into a large saucepan over a medium heat, add the garlic and thyme leaves with a big pinch of salt and cook for 1 minute. Next, add the onion and cook for another 2 minutes. Add in the celery and carrot, cooking for a further 10 minutes until soft, stirring occasionally.

Add the tomatoes and the vegetable stock or water and bring to the boil, then cover with a lid or plate, reduce to a simmer and cook for 20–30 minutes, stirring occasionally. Finish with basil, if you are using, and season generously with salt and pepper.

If you are preparing a pasta sauce, reduce the quantity of vegetable stock/water to 100ml/3½fl oz and proceed as above.

Meanwhile, make your sandwiches. Butter all 8 slices of bread on one side. Place 4 slices of bread, butter-side up, on a chopping board, top with the cheese slices, then spread over some pickle. Top with the remaining bread slices, butter-side down, to make 4 sandwiches. Cut each sandwich in half to serve.

Ladle the tomato soup into bowls, and serve the sandwiches alongside, together in perfect harmony.

Winter greens minestrone

A hearty Italian soup and a great one for using up leftovers such as cooked pasta, rice or noodles. Chickpeas work the best in our opinion, but other varieties of canned beans or pulses will also do. Start with your sofrito base (onion, celery, carrot) and build up your flavour as you progress – the trick is in the melding of ingredients as outlined below. Our Wild Garlic Pesto (see page 144) goes really well on top.

Serves 4

For the sofrito (soup base)
3 tbsp olive oil
2 garlic cloves, crushed
1 onion, diced
2 celery sticks, diced
2 carrots, washed and grated or diced
a pinch of salt

For the rest
200g/7oz winter greens, such as cavolo nero, Swiss chard or kale, leaves stripped off and finely chopped, stalks finely chopped
1 x 400g/14oz can tomatoes
800ml/28fl oz water or vegetable stock (home-made or stock cube options are fine)
1 x 400g/14oz can chickpeas or other beans
salt and freshly ground black pepper

To finish and serve
crusty bread
50g/1¾ oz freshly grated Parmesan cheese (optional)
olive oil or pesto

For the sofrito, put a large saucepan over a medium-high heat with the olive oil and garlic. Cook for 1 minute, then add the rest of your prepared sofrito vegetables and the pinch of salt.

Reduce the heat to medium and cook until everything is very soft, about 20–30 minutes, stirring occasionally. During cooking when the pan starts to stick, add a splash of water to loosen and continue to cook down further – this is what we call our 'melding' technique.

Add the winter greens stalks to the pot and cook for 5 minutes. Next, add the tomatoes, then fill the empty can with water twice (to get your measured water) and add this or the vegetable stock. Pour in the canned chickpeas or other beans, including their liquid, and bring back to a simmer, then cover with a lid and cook for another 20 minutes.

Add the remaining winter greens leaves, stir through and cook for another minute or two. Season to taste with salt and pepper.

Ladle into bowls and serve with some nice crusty bread. Sprinkle over the Parmesan, if you have some, and add some good-quality olive oil or pesto on top (try our Wild Garlic Pesto on page 144).

Dad's Scotch broth

This is a firm favourite in my dad's repertoire. He has soup every day for lunch and this one hits the spot, particularly during the Scottish winter months. It nourishes and fills while using basic vegetables and storecupboard ingredients. Best served on a cold day after working with your hands.

Serves 4–6

For the soup

2 large leeks, washed and thickly sliced
neutral or olive oil, for frying
5 medium potatoes, peeled and chopped into large chunks
3 carrots, washed and chopped into chunks
1 tsp freshly ground white or black pepper, plus extra to season at the end
1 tsp dried mixed herbs
2 vegetable stock cubes
50g/1¾oz pearl barley
75g/2¾oz dried yellow split peas, rinsed and drained
100g/3½oz dried red split lentils, rinsed and drained
2 bay leaves (if you're feeling fancy)
salt

To serve

1 loaf of crusty white bread, sliced
butter and mature Cheddar cheese (optional)

Into a large pot, add the leeks with a little neutral or olive oil and sweat over a medium heat until softened, about 5–7 minutes.

Add the potatoes and carrots and stir together. Add the ground pepper, a good pinch of salt and the dried herbs.

Crumble in the stock cubes (or use your own home-made vegetable stock) and mix with enough water to cover all the vegetables in the pot, plus a few cm/inches (about 2 litres/3½ pints). Stir in all the pulses and the bay leaves (if using).

Put a lid on, bring to the boil, then reduce the heat and simmer for 1 hour until the pulses and potatoes are cooked, stirring occasionally. Fish out the bay leaves (if using). You shouldn't need to blend any of the soup as the lentils will make it creamy. Season to taste with more salt and pepper.

Ladle the soup into bowls and enjoy with some crusty white bread, with lots of butter and some mature Cheddar, if you like.

Smoky sweetcorn and root vegetable chowder

One of my favourite soups is smoked haddock chowder. I cooked it for a client's lunch and someone asked for a vegan alternative. I came up with this version and was very pleased with the result. There's quite a bit of dicing involved, so it's good for practising your knife skills.

Makes 6

100g/3½oz dried yellow split peas
2 tbsp olive or coconut oil
1 onion, shallot or leek, finely diced
2 garlic cloves, finely chopped
3 celery sticks, finely diced
1 carrot, washed and grated or finely diced
500g/1lb 2oz either potatoes, celeriac or parsnips, scrubbed/peeled and cubed
1 tbsp smoked paprika
2 x 400g/14oz cans coconut milk
1 corn on the cob, kernels stripped, or 1 x 340g/11¾oz can sweetcorn, drained
1 red pepper, deseeded and finely diced
salt and freshly ground black pepper

Start by placing the lentils in a small bowl and covering them with cold water, then prepare all your vegetables.

Take a large pot, put it over a medium heat and add the olive or coconut oil, the onion, shallot or leek and the garlic with a pinch of salt and cook for 1 minute.

Next, add the celery and carrot and cook for 5 minutes, turning the heat down if it begins to stick. Add the diced potatoes or other root vegetable and 100ml/3½fl oz of water and cook for a further 10 minutes. Add the smoked paprika and stir for 1 minute.

Drain off and discard the soaking water from the lentils. Add the lentils into the pot and top up with 500ml/18fl oz of fresh water, then turn the heat up. When it boils, reduce the heat, cover with a lid and simmer for 15 minutes. The lentils should be fully cooked but, if not, simmer for another 5 minutes.

Now add both cans of coconut milk, the corn kernels or sweetcorn and the red pepper and bring gently to a simmer. Put the lid back on for 10 minutes, taking care to not let it boil.

Finish by seasoning to taste with salt and pepper. Ladle into bowls to serve.

Inside-out omelette

Instead of folding through the vegetables, herbs and cheese for a more traditional style omelette, this places all your ingredients on top of the omelette, centre stage. The soft, mild cheese is a perfect vehicle for the aromatic herbs, and makes for a pretty, colourful lunch. A great one for summer; slice up in wedges and serve with fried potatoes or a simple green salad.

Serves 4

100g/3½oz green beans, shelled peas or broad beans, or asparagus or ½ head of broccoli, chopped into small pieces
6–8 eggs
3 tbsp or 50ml/2fl oz milk (dairy or plant-based)
1 tbsp butter or olive oil, plus extra olive oil for drizzling
100g/3½oz ricotta, mascarpone cheese or thick, natural yogurt
1 tomato, chopped
3 spring onions, finely sliced
salt and freshly ground black pepper
a handful of chopped herbs, such as parsley, mint, coriander, dill, chervil, chives (or a mixture), to garnish
simple green salad or fried potatoes (see page 13), to serve (optional)

Put a pot of water on to boil with a pinch of salt. Blanch the green vegetables by cooking them in the boiling water for 1 minute. Drain and set aside to cool.

Whisk the eggs and milk together in a bowl and season with a pinch of salt.

Melt the butter or olive oil in your large, non-stick frying pan over a high heat. Pour in the egg mix and make the omelette by loosely stirring the eggs a few times in the pan, keeping the temperature high for about 30 seconds. Reduce the heat to medium-low and spread the egg around the whole pan to gently cook through underneath, about 2–3 minutes.

Once a little browned on the bottom and cooked through on top, turn off the heat and either slide the omelette on to a plate or serve in the pan. You can remove it from the pan by carefully shuffling the omelette to the edge and slipping a dinner plate underneath. Alternatively, you can use two large plates. Use the first one to cover the whole omelette and then carefully flip the pan over. Lift away the pan, then place the second plate over the upturned omelette. Flip again to present the omelette the right way up.

Now lightly spread the cheese or yogurt over the omelette and evenly scatter the tomato, spring onions and blanched green vegetables on top. Finish by garnishing with the herbs, seasoning to taste with salt and black pepper, then drizzling over a little olive oil. Cut into portions and serve on its own or with a simple green salad or fried potatoes (see page 13), if you like.

Smoked mackerel wrap with broccoli and toasted seeds

My uncle Tim, or Tim 'the Grybyn' as he's known in mid-Wales, went through a spell of making mackerel wraps for lunch every day, with ingredients purchased from the Morrisons supermarket next door to his office. We've added some embellishments here. We also eat this mackerel mix with salad plates, on toast or with baked potatoes.

Makes 2 large wraps

½ head of broccoli, washed with the core intact, sliced lengthways in 1cm/½ inch strips
2 tbsp pumpkin seeds and/or sunflower seeds
2 smoked mackerel fillets or other smoked fish, skinned and de-boned
4 spring onions, finely chopped (red or white onion will also work)
grated zest and juice of ½ lemon
4 tbsp mayonnaise or Greek-style yogurt (dairy or plant-based)
2 flour tortillas
a handful of rocket or baby spinach leaves, rinsed
salt and freshly ground black pepper

First, prepare your broccoli by frying the strips with a pinch of salt in a large, dry, non-stick frying pan over a high heat until a little charred, turning occasionally, about 2½ minutes on each side. Transfer to a bowl when done.

In the same pan, toast the seeds over a lower heat until they start to pop, about 1–2 minutes. Set aside in the same bowl.

To make the mackerel mix, flake the mackerel into a bowl, then add the spring onions. Add the lemon zest and juice and mayonnaise or yogurt, season generously with salt and pepper and stir together with a spoon.

Next, toast the tortillas, one at a time, in the same frying pan over a high heat on both sides until softened. Don't let them get crispy otherwise they will be hard to roll.

Assemble the wraps by spreading each one with the mackerel mix first. Layer in the leaves, followed by the charred broccoli, then the toasted seeds. Roll up and enjoy.

Kale Caesar

A twist on the original, we've adapted this using winter greens, such as kale, cavolo nero or rainbow chard. You could substitute the mackerel for smoked tofu and use nutritional yeast instead of cheese in the dressing, if you prefer a plant-based alternative. Use store-bought mayonnaise (dairy or plant-based) for the dressing, or better yet, make your own using the recipe on page 129. This is great as a side salad or as a lighter meal on a hot day.

Serves 2 as a light main or 4 as a side or starter

For the salad

1–3 tbsp olive oil
2 garlic cloves, crushed
1 sprig of thyme, leaves picked (optional)
2 slices of bread (sourdough is our preference), cubed
3 tbsp walnuts, roughly chopped
1 x 200g/7oz packet smoked tofu, drained and sliced, or 2 large smoked mackerel fillets, skinned and flaked into large pieces
1 x 200g/7oz packet kale, cavolo nero or rainbow chard, washed, leaves cut into bite-sized pieces and stalks finely sliced
salt

For the dressing

2 tbsp mayonnaise (dairy or plant-based)
grated zest and juice of 1 lemon
2 tbsp olive oil
1 small garlic clove, crushed
2 tbsp freshly grated Parmesan cheese or 1 tbsp nutritional yeast (optional)

For the salad, get your large, non-stick frying pan over a medium heat and pour in 1 tablespoon of olive oil, then add the garlic and thyme leaves and cook for 10 seconds. Add the bread cubes and fry in the oil for 5–7 minutes until golden brown, moving them around occasionally and adding in the walnuts for the last 2 minutes. Set aside in a bowl.

Keep your pan hot if you are using the smoked tofu, add another 2 tablespoons of olive oil to the pan and heat, then add the tofu slices and fry over a medium heat for 1–2 minutes on each side, until lightly browned and a little crispy. Remove to a plate and leave to cool, then cut into cubes.

Put the kale or other leaves in a large mixing or serving bowl and season with a pinch of salt.

For the dressing, mix the mayonnaise with the lemon zest and juice, the olive oil, garlic, a pinch of salt and the Parmesan or nutritional yeast (if using) in a small bowl.

Add the dressing to the leaves and mix together well. Fold in the flaked pieces of mackerel or your smoked tofu, the croutons and walnuts, then serve up.

Refried bean quesadillas with pico de gallo

Tex Mex at its best. Refried beans are a rich, earthy addition to a cheese quesadilla. We've included a method for the beans, but it would easily work with canned. There's not much to making your own, but a little patience goes a long way. This is ultimate comfort food, best washed down with a cold Michelada (see page 127) after a long walk or as a pre-dinner snack.

Makes 2 quesadillas

1 tbsp olive oil
½ small onion, diced
2 garlic cloves, chopped
a pinch of salt
1 tsp ground cumin
1 x 400g/14oz can beans or pulses of your choice (pinto beans are traditional)
4 large flour tortillas
200g/7oz mature Cheddar cheese, grated

For the pico de gallo
3 ripe tomatoes, finely chopped
½ red or white onion, finely diced
1 garlic clove, minced to a paste with a little salt
1 fresh chilli (any variety), finely chopped
a few coriander sprigs, finely chopped (optional)
a pinch of salt
grated zest and juice of 1 lime
2 tbsp olive oil

If you're making your refried beans, heat the olive oil in a saucepan over a medium heat, then fry the onion and garlic with a pinch of salt for 5–10 minutes until soft and translucent, stirring occasionally. Stir in the ground cumin and cook for another minute or so.

Add the beans along with their liquid and cook at a steady simmer, stirring occasionally, until reduced and thick, about 15–20 minutes. Crush the beans as much as possible in the pan with a fork until it becomes a thick paste. Remove from the heat and set aside to cool a little.

If using pre-made beans, open the can and stir the contents well.

Make your pico de gallo. Stir the tomatoes, onion, garlic, chilli, coriander (if using) and a pinch of salt together in a small bowl, then stir in the lime zest and juice and the olive oil. Set aside.

To make the quesadillas, lay the first tortilla out on a chopping board and spread half the bean paste all over it, then top generously with half the grated cheese and lay another tortilla on top. Repeat this to make the second quesadilla.

Ideally using a dry, heavy-based/cast-iron (or large, non-stick) frying pan, cook your quesadillas, one at a time, over a medium heat until browned and a little crispy on one side, about 5–10 minutes. Carefully flip over to cook

the other side. Once the cheese has fully melted, about 5–7 minutes, take the pan off the heat, rest for 1 minute or so and then remove and slice up into wedges. Cook and serve the second quesadilla in the same way. Enjoy with the pico de gallo as a dip alongside.

Kimchi cheese toastie

The salty, spicy fermented cabbage and the mature Cheddar works beautifully to create an umami flavour bomb. A chef's tip – toast longer on the cheese-side of your filled toastie because heating the kimchi past 46°C/115°F can kill the probiotic bacteria. Making your own kimchi is really rewarding, cost-effective and ready in just a few days in warm weather. Use the method below without kimchi for a regular cheese toastie, if you prefer.

Makes 2 toasties

3 tbsp (about 50g/1¾oz) butter, softened
4 slices of bread of your choice (sourdough is our preference)
200g/7oz mature Cheddar cheese, grated
5 tbsp (about 75g/2¾oz) kimchi
potato crisps and/or pickles, to serve

Spread the butter on one side of each slice of bread, then turn two slices over, butter-side down (you want the buttered sides on the outside of your sandwiches). Top with the grated cheese and kimchi, dividing them evenly between the two slices, then place the remaining two bread slices on top, butter-side up.

Put your large, non-stick frying pan over a medium heat (if you have a heavy-based/cast iron pan, this is best for toasties) and add your toastie, cheese-side down first (if you can fit both sandwiches in your pan, even better).

Cook gently over a medium-low heat until crisp and golden brown and the cheese has melted, about 5–10 minutes (the cooking times will depend on the type of bread and pan you use). Flip it over and quickly crisp up on the kimchi-side, about 3–5 minutes. Remove to a plate and repeat with the second sandwich, if necessary.

Slice each sandwich in half, then serve with some potato crisps, pickles or both, and a cold beer.

Spicy black bean tortilla soup

This is our version of 'tortilla soup', a deeply comforting dish with many layers. Traditionally, 'sopa de tortilla' comes from Mexico City and uses chicken broth, but I keep mine spicy and tomato-based with plenty of rich veg stock, black beans and vegetables. It might sound unusual at first, but the blend of richness and textures will make this a firm favourite for cosy days. Don't worry if you don't have all the toppings – the critical components in our opinion are coriander, yogurt, chillies and, of course, crispy tortillas.

Serves 4

For the base

1 red onion, diced
4 garlic cloves, chopped
2 celery sticks, diced
2 fresh chillies, red or green, finely chopped (seeds left in, depending on your heat preference), or 1 tsp cayenne pepper
½ small bunch of coriander, stalks finely chopped and leaves saved for garnish
2 tbsp olive oil
1 tbsp ground cumin
1 tsp smoked paprika
1 x 400g/14oz can tomatoes
2 x 400g/14oz cans black beans
2 vegetable stock cubes or 2 tsp vegetable bouillon/stock powder (optional)
1 corn on the cob, kernels stripped, or 1 x 340g/11¾oz can sweetcorn, drained
salt and freshly ground black pepper

For the garnishes

1 bag (about 200g/7oz) salted tortilla chips, or 4 corn or flour tortillas, cut into strips

For the base, in a large pot, sweat off the onion, garlic, celery, chillies and coriander stalks in the olive oil with a pinch of salt over a medium heat until soft, about 10 minutes or so.

Add the spices (including the cayenne pepper, if using instead of the chillies) and cook for a further minute. Add the tomatoes and stew for a further 2 minutes.

Add the black beans (including their liquid), 400ml/14fl oz of water, swilling it around in the tomato can, and the stock cubes or powder (if using). Bring back to the boil over a high heat, then reduce to a simmer, cover with a lid and cook for 20 minutes, stirring occasionally.

While the soup is simmering, prep your garnishes. If using tortillas instead of tortilla chips, fry them in batches. To do this, heat a little olive oil (about 1 tablespoon per batch) in a large, non-stick frying pan over a high heat, add a batch of tortilla strips and fry for 1–2 minutes, until browned and a little crispy. Scoop out on to a plate lined with kitchen paper and set aside to drain while you cook the rest in batches.

Add your corn kernels or sweetcorn to the soup and cook for 5 minutes if using fresh kernels or just add at the last minute if using canned. Season the soup to taste with salt and pepper and then spoon into bowls.

olive oil, for frying (optional)
100g/3½oz mature Cheddar cheese (or vegan cheese), grated
1 ripe avocado, peeled, stoned and diced (optional)
4 tbsp natural yogurt or soured cream (dairy or plant-based)
1 lime, cut into 4 wedges
1 fresh red or green chilli, thinly sliced (optional)

To finish, crack your tortilla chips or fried strips over the top of the soup and layer on your grated cheese, avocado (if using), coriander leaves (roughly chopped, if you like) and a dollop of yogurt or soured cream. Finish off with a squeeze of lime and some extra chilli, if you like it hot.

Tarka dhal

We can't think of a more satisfying, versatile and thrifty dish. The tarka here refers to spices fried up and stirred into the finished dish, and the dhal refers to the cooked lentils. We often have it for dinner with a baked potato, for breakfast on toast instead of beans, with a poached egg, or for lunch with greens. This dish looks like a lot of steps, but once you have the hang of it it's super easy and light on the washing up.

Serves 6–8

For the dhal

500g/1lb 2oz dried red split lentils
2 tbsp coconut or olive oil
2 red or brown onions, finely chopped
5 garlic cloves, chopped
a thumb-sized piece of fresh ginger, peeled and grated or chopped
2 tsp ground cumin
2 tsp ground turmeric
2 tsp ground coriander
2 tsp chilli flakes, or 2 fresh red or green chillies, chopped
1 x 400g/14oz can tomatoes, or 400g/14oz fresh tomatoes, chopped
1.25 litres/2¼ pints vegetable stock or water (see Chef's Tip)
salt
pitta bread or naan bread, to serve

For the tarka

2 tbsp coconut or olive oil
2 tsp cumin seeds
2 tsp coriander seeds
1 tbsp fresh or dried curry leaves (optional)

First, make the dhal. Start by placing the lentils in a container and covering them with cold water.

Next, put a large pot over a medium heat with the coconut or olive oil. Fry the onions for 5 minutes, then add the garlic and ginger with a pinch of salt and cook for a further 5 minutes.

Add in the ground spices and chilli flakes or chillies and cook for a further minute, stirring. Drain the soaked lentils and pour them into the pot along with the tomatoes and vegetable stock or water. Bring to the boil, then reduce to a very gentle simmer, cover and cook for 45–60 minutes, stirring occasionally, until the lentils are very soft and a nice consistency.

Meanwhile, to make the tarka, simply put a non-stick frying pan over a high heat. Add your coconut or olive oil, the spice seeds and the curry leaves (if using) and stir together for 30 seconds until the seeds are fragrant and popping (but make sure they don't burn!). If you prefer, you can omit this whole step and you'll still have a delicious dhal.

Heat your choice of pitta or naan bread (one or two at a time) in a large, dry, non-stick frying pan over a medium-high heat for 1–2 minutes until fully warmed through.

Pour the tarka (if using) into the dhal and stir through. Season the finished dish well with salt to taste. Serve with the warmed pitta or naan breads.

Chef's Tip

For a creamier dhal, replace 400ml/14fl oz of the vegetable stock/water with 1 x 400g/14oz can coconut milk, and add the coconut milk along with the stock/water as above.

You could add some shredded spinach leaves or leafy greens or even a 400g/14oz can chickpeas or pulses (drained) stirred through at the end, too, if you like.

Summer rolls with cheat's peanut satay sauce

I learned how to make summer rolls from my friend's mother, Mai Lan, who created the most wonderful Vietnamese dishes from her kitchen on Orcas Island. You can buy the rice paper from any Asian supermarket or online, and once you get the knack of the water preparation, they are super simple and fun to make. They keep well for picnics with a damp piece of kitchen paper on top to keep the rice paper fresh.

Makes 6 summer rolls

For the summer rolls

100g/3½oz dried thin rice noodles
a splash of sesame or olive oil (optional)
6 round sheets of rice paper (each 18cm/7 inches wide)
1 carrot, washed and sliced into finger-length thin strips like thick matchsticks
½ cucumber, sliced the same as the carrot
3 radishes, sliced (optional)
5 Little Gem lettuce leaves, finely chopped
6 sprigs of mint, leaves picked
6 sprigs of coriander, cut into thirds lengthways

For the cheat's peanut satay sauce

3 tbsp peanut butter (preferably smooth)
1 tbsp rice wine vinegar, or grated zest and juice of ½ lime
½ tsp white sugar
2 tsp soy sauce

First prep all the ingredients for the summer rolls and put in separate piles on a plate or in small containers.

For the peanut satay sauce, in a small dish, simply stir together the peanut butter with the vinegar or lime zest and juice, sugar, soy sauce and 1 tablespoon of water until fully incorporated and smooth. If it's a little thick, stir in a little more water. Set aside.

Cook the rice noodles according to the packet instructions. Drain, refresh with cold water, then drain again and leave in the pot. You can toss them with a little sesame or olive oil to prevent them from sticking together, if needed.

Take your first round of rice paper, then submerge it in a shallow dish of cold water for 1½ minutes or until fully pliable. Carefully take it out and place on a dry wooden chopping board or clean tea towel. Add a few of the noodles and a few pieces of each vegetable, lettuce and herbs to the middle of the rice paper round, arranging them neatly.

Next, roll up like a burrito, folding in the ends first, then the rest, packing tightly as you move upwards. Add a little more water with your finger when you get to the end if it's too dry and use it as glue to help it stick together, resting it seam-side down on the board. This takes some practice but even the messy ones are tasty, so keep going! Repeat for the remaining rolls.

To serve, cut the rolls (on the diagonal, if you like) in half or quarters and enjoy with the peanut satay dipping sauce.

Indonesian salad plate – Gado Gado

We were fortunate to travel to Indonesia a few years ago to volunteer with North Bali Reef Conservation in Tianyar. Making our way down south to surf, we ate at the local 'warungs' nearly every day. These roadside eateries serve up dishes in an all-day buffet, and Gado Gado was a firm favourite – it translates as 'mix mix' and is all brought together by the peanut satay sauce.

Serves 2 as a large salad plate

500g/1lb 2oz new potatoes, salad potatoes or sweet potatoes (washed and cut into chunks)
200g/7oz French beans, sugar snap peas, broccoli or asparagus, trimmed
4 eggs, or 1 x 200g/7oz packet tempeh, cut into strips
1 tbsp olive oil (if using tempeh)
2 portions of Cheat's Peanut Satay Sauce (see page 58)
200g/7oz dried rice noodles of your choice (optional)
2 heads of Little Gem or 1 head of Romaine lettuce, washed and leaves picked
salt

Put your potatoes in a large pot with a big pinch of salt and cover them with cold water, then bring to the boil and cook until tender (sweet potatoes take a little less time than regular potatoes). Remove from the pan with a slotted spoon and reserve the cooking water.

Add the green beans or vegetables to the water, topping it up if necessary, then bring back to the boil and cook for 1 minute. Remove from the pan to a plate with a slotted spoon, then set aside, reserving the water again.

Carefully add the eggs (if using) to the hot water and bring it back to the boil. Boil gently for 6½ minutes for soft-boiled eggs. Drain, plunge the eggs into cold water and leave until they are cool enough to handle, then peel off the shells and cut in half.

If you are using tempeh, heat the olive oil in a large, non-stick frying pan over a medium heat and cook for 2 minutes on each side until lightly browned.

Meanwhile, make the peanut satay sauce according to the recipe on page 58 and cook the rice noodles according to the packet instructions (see also page 12).

To serve, place the salad leaves on your plate (ripping any bigger leaves in half). Neatly arrange the rest of the ingredients around the dish. Either drizzle the satay sauce over the top or serve in a separate dish for dipping.

Triple nut trail mix

Pre-made bags of trail mix are fine in a pinch, but if you want to get more for your money, make your own and reduce plastic by buying nuts and dried fruit in bulk. Great for long plane journeys, hikes and other trips where you need regular boosts of energy. Add pieces of dark chocolate and a bag of pretzels for something really special.

Makes a 1.8kg/4lb bag (enough for a large group or for multiple trips for 2 people)

500g/1lb 2oz raw almonds
500g/1lb 2oz raw peanuts
250g/9oz raw cashew nuts
10 fresh medjool dates, stoned
1 x 200g/7oz bar milk or dark chocolate (optional)
250g/9oz raisins, dried mulberries or dried cherries
1 small bag (about 175g/6oz) salted pretzels

Roughly chop your nuts, dates and chocolate and mix together in a bowl or container along with the dried fruit. Throw in your pretzels and mix. Easy!

Store in an airtight container or jar or a sealed food/freezer bag at room temperature. This trail mix will keep for up to 6 weeks.

Chef's Tip

Toast your whole nuts in a frying pan first, if you prefer a stronger flavour. Simply toast them all together in a large, dry, non-stick frying pan (or in batches in a smaller pan) over a medium heat, moving them around the pan for 5–10 minutes or until lightly coloured, then leave to cool and roughly chop.

Date, peanut butter and cashew energy bombs

We started buying energy bars quite a bit when versions with unrefined sugar came on to the market. These are of course delicious, but if they're a regular snack, it's much more economical to invest in the ingredients upfront and make them yourself. This is easier if you have a food processor, but you can chop and mix them by hand, too. We make them in double or triple batches.

Makes 10 energy bombs

200g/7oz stoned fresh dates (ideally medjool), chopped
100g raw cashew nuts, finely chopped
100g peanut butter, crunchy or smooth, at room temperature

In a mixing bowl or large saucepan, mix all the ingredients together until combined, then, using your hands, divide and shape the mix into smooth, round balls, each about the size of a ping pong ball.

Place on a plate or tray and leave to set in the refrigerator overnight for best results. They'll keep in an airtight container in the refrigerator for about a week, or for up to 3 months, well-wrapped, in the freezer (make sure to thaw before eating).

Pick your popcorn

Hands down, popcorn is my number one favourite snack. The moreish texture and flavour possibilities take this ever-popular drinks accompaniment to another level. Make sure you turn the heat off immediately when you hear the pops slowing down – there is a fine line here between done and burning.

Serves 2

3 tbsp coconut, olive or neutral oil (coconut oil is our favourite)
4 tbsp popcorn kernels
1 tsp salt
selection of seasonings for savoury or sweet options, such as nutritional yeast, dried seaweed sprinkles, dukkah, za'atar, butter, freshly grated Parmesan cheese, chilli powder, cayenne pepper, coconut sugar, cinnamon sugar (made by combining 1 tbsp caster sugar with ½ tsp ground cinnamon)

Put a large pot over a medium-high heat and measure your oil and kernels into the pot.

Stir the kernels around so they get evenly coated in the oil and spread out on the bottom of the pan. Place a lid on top and set your timer.

It will take about 45 seconds for the pops to start. Try not to lift the lid, as this lets out heat (and kernels).

As soon as the pops slow down at around 2 minutes, 45 seconds, turn off the heat immediately and keep the lid on.

Mix the salt with 1 tablespoon of your preferred seasoning (½ teaspoon, if using the chilli powder or cayenne) in a small bowl. If using the butter, melt it first in a small saucepan.

Remove the lid, pour the seasoning over the popcorn, tossing to mix well and seasoning the popcorn evenly, then transfer to bowls for sharing.

DINNER

Cinnamon rosewater pilaf with raisins and almonds

I would often cook this for Karakusevic Carson Architects (KCA), where I worked as a private chef for four years. We'd serve it up family-style on two big wooden tables in the office. Lots of soups, stews, curries and pies in the winter, and salads, quiches, tapas, antipasti and mezze in the summer. I'd make this pilaf rice to go with curries rather than just plain rice. This was one of the autumn favourites and can be a meal in itself. Serve as a main meal or an accompaniment with a curry. You will need a circle of greaseproof paper for this recipe.

Serves 4

250g/9oz basmati rice (we always use the Tilda brand)
2 onions, thinly sliced
4 garlic cloves, thinly sliced
2 tbsp olive oil
1 tsp ground cinnamon
1 tbsp rosewater
50g/1¾oz raisins or currants
450ml/16fl oz boiling water or vegetable stock
a big pinch of salt

To serve
50g/1¾oz raw almonds, chopped (optional)
4 tbsp Greek-style natural yogurt (optional)
a bunch of coriander, leaves stripped (optional)

First, soak the rice in cold water for 30 minutes, then drain.

Next, fry the onions and garlic with the olive oil in a large pot over a medium heat, stirring frequently, until brown and sticky, about 25 minutes. If the mix is catching on the bottom of the pan, add a splash of water to deglaze and then continue caramelizing.

When the mix is really soft and sticky, add the cinnamon, rosewater and raisins or currants and stir everything together. Cook for another minute, then add the soaked rice and the hot water or vegetable stock and the big pinch of salt.

Stir, bring to the boil, then reduce to a simmer, cover with a circle of greaseproof paper (plus a lid if you have one) and cook for about 15 minutes, without stirring. Check the rice on the top is cooked, then turn off the heat and let the pot rest with the lid on (without stirring) for a final 5–10 minutes.

Stir through the pilaf, then plate up and serve with the chopped almonds, yogurt and some coriander, if you like.

Budget supermarket pasta for 4

This is our go-to pasta dish if we're in a pinch, on a budget or have limited options at our disposal. You should be able to get all these ingredients from a corner shop, garage or small supermarket. The important part is to spend time sweating down the base – we call this 'melding'. Another tip is to save some of the pasta water to make an emulsion with the oily sauce at the end. You can omit the anchovies and Parmesan to make a plant-based version, if you prefer.

Serves 4

4 tbsp olive oil, plus an extra splash
2 red onions, thinly sliced
8 garlic cloves, thinly sliced
1 fresh red chilli (seeds left in, depending on heat preference) or 1 tbsp chilli flakes
5–6 canned anchovy fillets in oil, drained (optional)
500g/1lb 2oz dried pasta, such as fusilli, penne or rigatoni
1 head of broccoli, stalk and florets cut into small pieces
salt and freshly ground black pepper
2 tbsp freshly grated Parmesan cheese or nutritional yeast, to garnish (optional)

Put a pot of salted water on to boil and move on to make the sauce.

Add the olive oil to a large, non-stick frying pan and sweat the onion, garlic, chilli and anchovies (if using) with a pinch of salt over a medium heat until very soft, about 15–20 minutes in total. During this sweating process, it doesn't matter if the mix browns a little; just add in a splash of water, then continue cooking, sweating down until the onion mixture starts to stick. Add a splash of water to deglaze and reduce again, repeating several times during the 15–20 minutes until the onion mixture is like a rich paste. They refer to this as 'in umido' in Italian, which roughly translates as steam cooking, and which we affectionately call 'melding'.

Meanwhile, add the pasta to the pot of boiling water along with the splash of olive oil and cook according to the packet instructions until al dente. Drain and set aside in the cooking pot, saving half a cupful of the pasta water.

Add the chopped broccoli stalk to the onion mixture with a splash of the reserved pasta water to help it steam-fry, moving it around in the pan for about a minute until softened, then add the florets and repeat again until vibrant green and tender.

Stir in the pasta and the remaining reserved pasta water and mix together with tongs or a spoon. Season to taste with salt and pepper, if desired.

Plate up and garnish with grated Parmesan or nutritional yeast (if using), or enjoy as it is.

Vietnamese pancakes

These light and crispy pancakes are dairy- and gluten-free and true to the original recipe, made with coconut milk and rice flour. Top with your choice of tofu, mushrooms or pork mince, and finish with some fresh herbs and a zing of lime.

Makes 4 large pancakes and filling

For the pancake batter
200g/7oz rice flour
200ml/7fl oz warm water
260ml/9¼ fl oz canned coconut milk, mixed well
4 spring onions, finely sliced
1 tsp ground turmeric (optional)
½ tsp salt
4 tsp coconut or olive oil

For the filling
½ banana shallot or onion, finely diced
a thumb-sized piece of fresh ginger, peeled and grated
2 garlic cloves, minced
1 tbsp coconut or olive oil
a big pinch of salt
1 tsp ground turmeric
1 x 350g/12oz packet firm tofu, drained and crushed with a fork, or 500g/1lb 2oz mushrooms, diced (for vegetarians and vegans), or 300g/10½ oz free-range pork mince
1 tsp fish sauce, or juice of ½ lime and a little salt

For the vegetables and herbs
1 large or 2 small carrots, washed and grated
½ cucumber, finely sliced
½ bunch of mint, leaves picked, left whole or torn into pieces
½ bunch of coriander, chopped

To finish
Nam Jim Sauce (see page 132) or ready-made hot chilli sauce
1 lime, cut into wedges

First make the nam jim sauce according to the recipe on page 132, or just have some chilli sauce ready to go.

For the pancake batter, whisk the rice flour, warm water and coconut milk together in a bowl or jug until smooth. Add the spring onions, turmeric (if using) and salt. You want the consistency of single cream, so add a little more coconut milk or water if needed. Set aside to rest at room temperature or in the refrigerator for at least 10 minutes before using.

For the filling, in your large, non-stick frying pan, fry the shallot or onion, ginger and garlic in the tablespoon of coconut or olive oil with the big pinch of salt over a medium heat for 2 minutes. Add the turmeric and either the tofu, mushrooms or pork mince and fry over a high heat for about 10 minutes, stirring frequently, until the mushrooms or pork mince have shrunk and released their juices or the tofu has coloured. Season to taste with fish sauce or lime juice and salt. Remove from the heat, transfer to a bowl, set aside and keep warm. Wipe out your frying pan.

Meanwhile, prep your vegetables and herbs and set aside.

Whisk the batter mix again, then cook the pancakes, one at a time by adding 1 teaspoon of the coconut or olive oil to your frying pan. Cover the bottom of the pan with a quarter of the batter, swirling it around the pan, then fry over a high heat, flipping it over halfway through (being careful not to break it!), until cooked on both sides and crispy on the underside, about 1½ minutes on each side. Transfer to a plate and keep warm. Repeat until you've used all the batter to make four large pancakes, whisking the batter in between batches.

Now fill the pancakes with the tofu, mushrooms or pork mix, then top with the carrots, cucumber and herbs. Fold and dress with the nam jim sauce or chilli sauce and serve with a wedge of lime on the side.

Amok peanut vegetable curry

My adaptation of this classic Cambodian dish. Typically made with white fish, the base lends itself well to a plant-based version with the addition of peanut butter to thicken the sauce. This will be a little quicker if you have a mini food processor to make the curry paste, but if you don't have the kit, take a jam jar and the end of a wooden spoon or a thin bottle to bash the paste together like in a pestle and mortar (or use a pestle and mortar if you have one to hand). The salt will help break down the ingredients.

Serves 4

For the base

4 garlic cloves, finely chopped
2 thumb-sized pieces of fresh ginger, peeled and grated or finely chopped
2 fresh green or red chillies (seeds left in), finely chopped
1 shallot, finely diced
2 tbsp coconut or olive oil
salt

For the curry

3 lemon grass stalks
2 carrots, washed and thinly sliced
8 kaffir lime leaves, or peeled zest of 1 lime
½ cauliflower, leaves removed and set aside, the rest (including the stalk) cut into florets
2 tbsp smooth peanut butter
2 tsp ground turmeric
2 x 400g/14oz cans coconut milk
100g/3½oz green beans, chopped, or frozen (thawed) or podded fresh peas
2 tbsp fish sauce, or juice of 2 limes and a little salt

To serve

300g/10½oz rice (any type) or 400g/14oz dried noodles of your choice (optional)
1 lime, cut into wedges

To garnish (optional)

fresh coriander sprigs, chopped
sliced fresh red chilli or dried chilli flakes

Start by bashing your base ingredients (garlic, ginger, chillies and shallot) together with a good pinch of salt (see intro). You'll end up with a thick, chunky paste.

Put a large pot over a medium heat and add the coconut or olive oil with another pinch of salt. Cook your paste along with the whole lemon grass stalks for about 5 minutes.

Add your carrots to the paste with the kaffir lime leaves or zest. Add 100ml/3½fl oz of water, reduce the heat to low and cook for 10 minutes, stirring occasionally. If you're cooking rice or noodles, now is a good time. Cook them according to the packet instructions, then drain and set aside, covered.

Add your cauliflower florets and stalk to the pot and cook over a low heat for another 10 minutes, stirring occasionally. Stir in your peanut butter and turmeric.

Next, pour in the coconut milk and 200ml/7fl oz of water and turn the heat up to high. As soon as it boils, reduce the heat to low. If it overheats, the coconut milk will split and you'll lose your nice creamy consistency.

Take the lemon grass out, then add in the chopped cauliflower leaves and green beans or peas. Simmer gently for 2 minutes. Season with the fish sauce or the lime juice and salt.

Serve with your finished rice or noodles (if using), a wedge of lime for each person and then garnish with the coriander and chilli (if using).

Chickpea pancakes with cauliflower and tomato salad

Chickpea flour, also known as gram or besan flour, is underrated, versatile and gluten-free and it is commonly used in Italian and Indian cuisine. You can find it in most supermarkets or Indian shops. Make the batter with chopped spinach, tomato, onion and Indian spices, and serve the pancakes with a crisp raw cauliflower salad, topped with fried eggs and chilli flakes for a healthy, energizing dish.

Serves 4

For the batter
250g/9oz chickpea flour
½ red onion, finely diced
1 tomato, diced
6 sprigs of coriander, finely chopped
2 tsp ground turmeric
2 tsp ground cumin
2 tsp chilli flakes or ½ fresh red chilli, finely chopped
1 tsp nigella seeds, toasted (optional) – see Chef's Tip
50g/1¾oz spinach leaves, chopped
½ tbsp salt
2 tbsp coconut or olive oil, for frying

For the salad
½ small cauliflower, halved, leaves and core removed, florets sliced wafer thin
¼ red onion, sliced
1 tomato, thinly sliced
100g/3½oz spinach leaves, chopped
6 sprigs of coriander, leaves picked
6 sprigs of mint, leaves picked (optional)
1 tsp chilli flakes, plus extra to serve
1 tsp salt
1 tbsp olive oil
juice of 1 lemon or lime

To finish
1 tbsp olive oil, plus extra to serve
4 eggs
salt and freshly ground black pepper

For the batter, put the chickpea flour in a bowl with the onion, tomato, coriander and all the spices. Mix in 400ml/14fl oz of water until completely smooth. Stir in the spinach and salt, then cover and leave to rest at room temperature or in the refrigerator for at least 10 minutes (and up to 2 hours).

Prepare the salad while the batter is resting. Mix the cauliflower, onion, tomato, spinach, coriander and mint (if using) with the chilli flakes, salt, olive oil and lemon or lime juice until combined. Set aside to marinate while you cook the pancakes.

Recipe continued from p.75

Put your large, non-stick frying pan over a medium-high heat and add ½ tablespoon (per pancake) of coconut or olive oil. Pour in a quarter of the pancake batter (it should sizzle), then cook until golden brown on the first side, about 2 minutes. To flip, carefully place a plate over the pan and turn it over, then slide the pancake back into the pan to cook on the other side for 1–2 minutes. Transfer to a plate and cover with a clean tea towel to keep it warm. Repeat with the remaining batter to make four pancakes in total.

To finish, add the olive oil (or butter, if you prefer) to your frying pan and quickly fry the eggs to your liking (we think a runny yolk is best).

To serve, put the pancakes on serving plates and divide up the dressed cauliflower and tomato salad. Top with the fried eggs, finish with extra chilli flakes and a drizzle of olive oil and season to taste with salt and pepper.

Chef's Tip *Toast nigella seeds in a dry, non-stick frying pan over a medium heat for about 1 minute or until fragrant.*

Corn tacos with shredded jackfruit

Meat eaters won't have any complaints if you serve them these tacos. I'd recommend using small corn tortillas as opposed to the flour variety for a more authentic flavour. It's worth buying a large packet and keeping them at home in the freezer.

Makes 8 small (10cm/4 inch) tacos for 2 people

For the jackfruit mix

1 tbsp olive or neutral oil
2 red onions, thinly sliced
4 garlic cloves, finely sliced
1 tbsp ground cumin
1 tbsp smoked paprika
1 tsp chilli powder, plus (optional) extra to serve
2 tsp dried oregano
1 tbsp tomato purée
1 tbsp molasses, date syrup or other sweetener
1 x 400g/14oz can jackfruit
salt

For the garnishes

1 ripe avocado, peeled, stoned and diced
1 quantity Pico de Gallo (see page 50) or 1 x 300g/10½oz jar tomato salsa
2 tbsp chopped jalapeño chillies (jarred varieties work well)
4 sprigs of coriander, chopped
1 lime, cut into 8 pieces

To serve

8 soft corn tortillas

First, make the filling by adding the olive or neutral oil to a pot with the onions, garlic and a pinch of salt. Sweat over a medium heat for 7 minutes, stirring to make sure the onions don't stick. Add a little water if needed.

Add in all the spices, the oregano, tomato purée, your sweetener and another big pinch of salt. Stir together, cooking for a further minute. Open the can of jackfruit and discard the liquid. Break it up with a fork until a little shredded, seeds and all, then add it to the pot along with 200ml/7fl oz of water and keep stirring.

Bring the mixture to the boil, then reduce to a simmer. Cook and reduce to a nice thick consistency that won't run out of the tacos, stirring occasionally, about 5–7 minutes. Season to taste with salt and some more chilli powder if you like it hot! You can make this in advance, then cool and store in an airtight tub in the refrigerator for up to 5 days. Reheat it gently in a pan until piping hot when you're ready for the tacos.

Prepare all your garnishes and get everything ready for assembling the tacos.

Fry your tortillas, one at a time, in a large, dry, non-stick frying pan over a high heat for about 30 seconds on each side or until a little coloured but not crispy. Transfer to a plate and keep warm while you cook the rest.

Assemble in the following order: corn tortilla, jackfruit mix, diced avocado, pico de gallo or salsa, chopped jalapeños, then the coriander and a drizzle of lime. Fold the tacos in half and enjoy with a Michelada (see page 127).

Egg-fried rice

You'll never attempt egg-fried rice another way once you've tried this method. Instead of scrambling the egg in the rice and vegetables (which can sometimes have disappointing results), you make an omelette first, chop it up and fold it through the stir-fry at the end. Stir-fries are excellent for using up leftovers and taste best made with day-old rice, it soaks up the flavours and fries better. So make extra the night before!

Serves 2

For the stir-fry

250g/9oz cooked cold basmati rice, day-old (or 150g/5½oz raw basmati rice)
½ bunch of spring onions, finely chopped
3 garlic cloves, finely chopped
a small knob of fresh ginger, peeled and finely chopped or grated
2 tbsp coconut, sesame or neutral oil
1 carrot, washed and grated
200g/7oz mushrooms, chopped
1 head of broccoli, chopped into small pieces, including stalk
juice of 1 lime
a handful of leafy greens, such as kale, chard or spinach, stalks and leaves separated and roughly chopped, or about 100g/3½oz any leftover cooked cold vegetables, finely chopped
2 tbsp fish sauce, or juice of 2 limes and a little salt
1 tbsp soy sauce
a small bunch of coriander, roughly chopped (optional)
1 tsp chilli flakes or 1 small fresh red chilli, deseeded and finely chopped
salt

For the omelette

4–6 eggs
1 tbsp soy sauce
1 tbsp butter

If you are cooking raw rice, cook and prepare it following the instructions on page 12.

To cook the omelette, whisk the eggs together with the soy sauce. Put your large, non-stick frying pan or wok over a high heat. Add the butter, then pour in the egg mixture, stirring it in the pan to scramble it slightly, about 30 seconds, then reduce the heat to medium-low and cook, without stirring, until the omelette is coloured on the bottom. Your omelette is done when it's almost fully cooked but still runny in the middle.

Fold in half and slide out on to a plate, then cool slightly before chopping up to be added to the stir-fry later.

Using the same pan, stir-fry half the spring onions, the garlic and ginger in the oil with a pinch of salt over a medium-high heat for 2 minutes. Reduce the heat to medium, then add the carrot, stir-frying for 1 minute. Add in the mushrooms and stir-fry for a further 2 minutes.

Turn the heat back up to high. Add the broccoli with the lime juice and stir-fry for another 2 minutes. Add the stalks of the leafy greens and cook for 30 seconds.

Now add the cooked rice and the chopped green leaves or leftover cooked veg. Stir-fry everything around in the pan for a few minutes to fully combine and heat through.

Finish by folding through the chopped omelette, then season with the fish sauce or lime juice/salt mix and the soy sauce. Sprinkle with the rest of the spring onions and the coriander (if using). Add the chilli flakes or chopped chilli to finish, then serve.

Rainbow rice bowl

Rainbow bowls are inspired by a Japanese dish called 'chirashi', which translates as 'scattered'. We've used chirashi as inspiration for a satiating vegan or vegetarian dish with lots of vibrant seasonal vegetables, pickles and an optional soft-boiled egg on top (we've also included a couple of other options, if you are meat/fish-eaters). The punchy dressing ties it all in.

Serves 2

For the rice

1½ tbsp rice wine vinegar (if using sushi rice)
1 tbsp white sugar (if using sushi rice)
200g/7oz sushi rice or other rice such as white basmati or short-grain brown rice
½ tsp salt

For the rest

½ red onion, thinly sliced
¼ cucumber, sliced
a small bunch of radishes, sliced, or 1 carrot, washed and sliced into strips
juice of 1 lime
a pinch of sugar
about 300g/10½oz seasonal vegetables such as broccoli, cauliflower, green beans, squash, asparagus (or a combo), chopped into large chunks or bite-sized pieces
2 eggs, or 1 x 200g/7oz packet fried tofu or tempeh, or your choice of meat, such as chicken, beef or pork (about 200g/7oz) or smoked fish (1 fillet)
1 tbsp olive oil (optional)
salt

To finish

Soy and Ginger Salad Dressing (see page 130), to taste
Seaweed Sprinkle (see page 131), to taste (optional)

If using sushi rice, mix the rice wine vinegar and sugar in a small bowl and set aside. Prepare your sushi rice first by rinsing your rice thoroughly in cold water – this first step gets rid of the starch. Put your sushi rice in a saucepan with 250ml/9fl oz of cold water and the salt and bring to the boil, then reduce the heat, cover with a lid and simmer for 10 minutes. Turn off the heat. Pour over the vinegar and sugar mix, stir through, then cover again.

Otherwise, cook your other rice as per the cooking instructions on page 12.

Recipe continued from p.82

While the rice is cooking, pickle your red onion, cucumber and radishes or carrot in a bowl by mixing them with the lime juice, pinch of sugar and a pinch of salt. Set aside.

Make the dressing and seaweed sprinkle (if using) to finish, according to the recipes on pages 130 and 131.

Put a second pan of water on to boil (about 500ml/18fl oz) with a pinch of salt. Blanch your prepped vegetables in the boiling water for 1 minute until just tender, then drain and set aside (reserve the hot water if using eggs).

Now prepare your protein. If using eggs, soft-boil your eggs for 6½ minutes in the hot vegetable water, then plunge into cold water and peel once cool (halve to serve). Alternatively, fry your tofu/tempeh/meat/fish in the olive oil in a large, non-stick frying pan over a high heat until browned and cooked to your liking (make sure the chicken and pork is cooked through, if using), or brush with oil and cook under a hot grill.

To assemble and serve, put the cooked rice in the bowls first, keeping it to one side, then add the vegetables. Add your choice of protein and then garnish with the pickles (juices and all). Drizzle over the dressing and scatter over the seaweed sprinkle (if using).

Tofu scramble

This scramble works well as a breakfast, lunch or dinner and scales down nicely as a side for a curry or dhal. It's super easy to make and a great way to liven up tofu if you're looking for different ways to enjoy it. The greens and kimchi together lend a juicy, spicy kick to the dish.

Serves 2

200g/7oz short-grain brown rice
1 x 350g/12oz packet firm tofu, drained
1 tsp ground turmeric
1 tbsp sesame, coconut or neutral oil
½ onion, diced
2 garlic cloves, chopped
a large knob of fresh ginger, peeled and grated or finely chopped
1 fresh green chilli, finely diced (optional)
10 sprigs of coriander, stalks finely chopped and leaves roughly chopped
a pinch of salt
1 tbsp fish sauce, or juice of 1 lime and a little salt

To serve
300g/10½oz seasonal leafy greens, roughly chopped
1 tbsp coconut or olive oil
a pinch of salt
2 generous spoonfuls of kimchi

Prepare and cook your rice according to the instructions on page 12.

While the rice is simmering, break up the tofu in a bowl using a fork, season with the turmeric and mix together.

Put a large, non-stick frying pan over a high heat and add in the oil. Once hot, add the onion, garlic, ginger, chilli and coriander stalks with a pinch of salt and fry for 3–5 minutes, moving everything evenly around the pan.

Next, add the tofu, cooking and moving it around the pan for a further 7 minutes until coloured and a little crispy. Add the chopped coriander leaves and season with the fish sauce or lime juice and salt, then set aside in a bowl and keep warm until you are ready to plate up.

Now cook your seasonal greens in the same pan with the coconut or olive oil, a pinch of salt and a splash of water with a lid on over a medium-high heat for about 1 minute.

Serve the tofu scramble with your cooked brown rice and seasonal greens and a generous spoonful of kimchi on top of each portion.

BBQ fish parcel

Also known as 'hobo' packets in the US, this is a really fun way of cooking on a campfire (that also saves on the washing up). All you have to do is mix your ingredients and seasonings together in a foil parcel, fold it up and place it carefully in the embers on the edge of the fire. Cooking times will vary – the trick is to get the embers even and smouldering first. You will need four large pieces of foil for this recipe.

Serves 2

4 spring onions, roughly chopped
2 garlic cloves, finely chopped
a small knob of fresh ginger, peeled and sliced into thin strips or grated
2 skinless white fish fillets, such as hake or sea bass, about 200g/7oz each
2 tbsp olive or sesame oil
2 tbsp soy sauce
1 lime, cut into quarters
2 pak choi, split in half lengthways, or use 200g/7oz broccoli florets or green beans
salt and freshly ground black pepper
cooked rice or noodles of your choice, to serve
a small handful of chopped herbs, such as dill or coriander, to garnish (optional)

Start by making two foil envelopes. Lay out a square piece of foil, approximately 45 x 45 cm (18 x 18 inches). Fold in half, and make three tight creases on each side (left and right). Turn over and make three similar tight creases on the bottom. Open the top to form an envelope for your ingredients and then repeat this process to make a second envelope.

Mix together the spring onions, garlic and ginger and place half in the bottom of each foil envelope, then lay a fish fillet on top and season with salt and pepper. Drizzle 1 tablespoon of olive or sesame oil over each fish fillet, followed by 1 tablespoon of soy sauce, then squeeze a lime quarter over each (leaving the lime shell in there, too). Lay the pak choi or other green veg over the fish.

Wrap up the parcels by closing each envelope tightly around the ingredients, then wrap each parcel with another large piece of foil.

Carefully place the parcels on a grill over some hot embers or directly on top of some coals. Refer to the guide on page 15 to help you know when the coals are ready.

Use some tongs if necessary and leave the parcels to cook for 10–12 minutes, shifting them around a couple of times to keep them on hot coals – you should hear the ingredients sizzling away in the parcels.

When you're satisfied the fish is cooked, carefully pour all the contents out of each parcel and straight into a serving bowl (discard the lime shells). Serve with cooked rice or noodles and garnish with chopped fresh herbs and the remaining lime wedges for squeezing over.

Isle of Wight fish stew

This dish is one of our all-time favourites for the van and has been honed for a small kitchen, using only one pot. We decided to cook this on the Isle of Wight one year on a camp stove when we couldn't find anything open except a fishmonger and a convenience store. It has been dubbed the Isle of Wight stew ever since. The original recipe hails from my time at The Dogs in Edinburgh and was taught to me by the head chef, Jamie Ross, who now runs a seafood truck in Inverness. Seek him out if you're up that way.

Serves 4

For the stew

a glug of olive oil, plus extra for drizzling
1 onion, cut into large dice
2 garlic cloves, crushed
1 leek, washed and chopped into chunks
2 carrots, washed and chopped into chunks
2 celery sticks, chopped into chunks
1 tsp tomato purée
50ml/2fl oz white wine
2 x 400g/14oz cans tomatoes
2 bay leaves
400g/14oz mixed skinless white fish fillets (ideally from a small day boat or choose the most sustainable options available), such as hake and monkfish, cut into even dice
500g/1lb 2oz fresh mussels in shell, de-bearded (see Chef's Tip on page 95) and rinsed well under cold water (discard any that don't close when tapped sharply)
salt and freshly ground black pepper

To finish and serve

a small handful of chopped soft herbs, such as parsley, dill, chervil, coriander, chives
soft white bread or baguette and butter (optional)

In a large pot, add a big glug of olive oil with the onion, garlic, leek, carrots, celery and a big pinch of salt and sweat down over a medium heat, stirring occasionally, for 20 minutes until you can gently squish the carrots with your spoon.

Add the tomato purée and cook for another minute, stirring. Pour in the white wine and reduce by half. Next, add the tomatoes, bay leaves and 200ml/7fl oz of water. Bring back to the boil, then reduce the heat, cover with a lid or plate on top and simmer for another 20 minutes.

Season the diced fish generously with salt and pepper. Add the fish to the pot, cover and cook for another 5 minutes, then add all your mussels to the same pot and cover again. Give the pan a good shake from side to side, then simmer for 5 minutes or so. Stir through carefully and make sure the mussels have all opened up. Cook for a little longer, if needed. Turn off the heat and discard any mussels that remain closed. Fish out the bay leaves.

Finish with the chopped herbs and stir them through once, being careful not to break up the fish. Season to taste with salt and a drizzle of olive oil and enjoy with some soft white bread or baguette and butter, if you like.

Pan-fried mackerel with herb and green olive crushed new potatoes

I caught my first mackerel while working at a five-star hotel in St. David's on the west coast of Wales during the summer of 2008. One day, I asked the hotel caretaker about mackerel fishing. He told me where the best beach was, including the precise rock. Some of the other chefs and I borrowed a cheap rod and some feathers and headed off. Second cast and I was in with a haul. We snuck back into the restaurant kitchen after service that night, after the head chef and all the staff had left, and cooked it up. There's always 'a' fishing spot; you just have to ask the locals.

Serves 2

500g/1lb 2oz new potatoes
a splash of olive oil
2 whole mackerel, about 250g/9oz each, filleted (skin on)
2 tbsp butter or olive oil
a small handful of soft herbs, such as parsley, dill, chives (or a mixture), chopped
2 spring onions, finely sliced
1 tbsp capers, drained
2 tbsp stoned green olives, chopped (Gordal are our favourites)
grated zest and juice of 1 lemon
salt and freshly ground black pepper

Add the potatoes to a pot of cold water with a big pinch of salt, then bring to the boil and cook until tender. Drain and keep warm in the same pan.

Get a large, non-stick frying pan smoking hot and add a splash of olive oil, then add the mackerel fillets, skin-side down, and reduce the heat to medium-high. Fry until cooked almost all of the way through, about 6 minutes. Turn the heat down a little if the skin is getting too dark, but don't move the fillets in the pan.

While the mackerel is cooking, lightly crush your potatoes in their pot with a fork. Stir through the butter or olive oil, then add the herbs, spring onions, capers and olives. Stir through half the lemon juice and all the zest, then season to taste with salt and pepper.

Finish the mackerel by flipping it over to cook for the last 10 seconds or so, squeezing over the remaining lemon juice.

To plate up, make a mound of crushed potatoes on each plate and top with the fried mackerel fillets and all the pan juices. Serve with wilted leafy greens or a side salad for a more substantial meal.

Date night tagliatelle

This dish has become a firm favourite of ours. It's a classic combo of smoked fish, cream and dill. Serve with plenty of cracked black pepper and a glass of chilled white wine. You can find smoked trout in a number of farm shops, delis and fishmongers, but you could also use smoked salmon or mackerel, if you prefer.

Serves 2

1 courgette
1 tbsp olive oil, plus an extra splash
2 garlic cloves, thinly sliced
½ banana shallot or small onion, thinly sliced
250g/9oz dried tagliatelle, spaghetti or fettuccine
50ml/2fl oz white wine (optional)
300ml/10fl oz double cream (dairy or plant-based)
½ a small bunch of dill, stalks finely chopped and leaves chopped
300g/10½ oz skinless hot or cold smoked trout or salmon fillets, flaked
salt and freshly ground black pepper
freshly grated Parmesan cheese or nutritional yeast, to finish (optional)

Put a large pot of water on to boil for the pasta and add 2 teaspoons of salt.

Prepare your courgette by cutting it in half widthways then slicing or peeling it into thin pasta-like strips to mimic the pasta, either using a mandoline or a vegetable peeler, if available. Set aside.

Now, take out a second pot, place it over a medium heat, add your olive oil, garlic and a pinch of salt and cook for 1 minute, then add the shallot or onion and cook gently for 5 minutes without colouring. Add a splash of water to the pan if it starts to colour.

Meanwhile, add the splash of olive oil and your pasta to the pot of salted boiling water and cook according to the packet instructions until al dente.

While the pasta finishes cooking, turn the heat on your onion and garlic back up to medium and add the white wine, if using. Reduce it by half, then add the cream, otherwise, just add the cream and bring to the boil. Drain the cooked pasta, saving a cupful of the pasta water.

Now, add the dill (stalks and leaves), courgette and flaked fish to the larger pot along with the cream sauce and the pasta. Bring back to a simmer, stirring with some tongs, and adjust the consistency using the reserved pasta water. Season with salt and a generous amount of pepper.

Divide the pasta between two bowls and finish with some Parmesan or nutritional yeast, if you like.

Mussels with samphire and pan-fried garlic bread

Mussels are considered an excellent sustainable source of protein. Unlike farmed fish, they don't require a feed and are natural filters for the waters they grow in (they are usually grown on ropes). They are also delicious with a multitude of sauces and super quick to cook up. If you'd like a gluten-free alternative as an accompaniment, pick up some fresh chips from a local shop, if there's one near you.

Serves 2

For the garlic bread

3 garlic cloves, peeled
a pinch of salt
2 tbsp butter, softened
3 tbsp roughly chopped parsley leaves (optional)
1 x 15cm/6 inch ciabatta loaf

For the mussels

1 tbsp butter or olive oil
1 banana shallot, thinly sliced
a pinch of salt
1kg/2lb 4oz fresh mussels in shell, de-bearded (see Chef's Tip) and rinsed well under cold water (discard any that don't close when tapped sharply)
100g/3½oz marsh samphire, tough ends picked off (this can usually be found on the south-east coast of England from May onwards – see page 149 – or bought from larger supermarkets or your fishmonger)
200ml/7fl oz white wine
freshly ground black pepper

First, prepare your garlic bread by finely mincing the garlic with a pinch of salt to form a paste. Mix with the butter and chopped parsley. Make six evenly-spaced widthways cuts in the ciabatta, almost through to the bottom, then spread some of the garlic butter on to one side of each slice of bread between each cut.

Fan out the bread a little in a large, non-stick frying pan so the heat gets into the buttered slices, it will want to close but don't worry too much. Then place a lid or mixing bowl on top or cover tightly with foil. Cook over a very low heat for 3–5 minutes. Take the bowl or foil 'lid' off carefully and flip the bread on to the other side, then cook for another 3–5 minutes until crispy and browned on both sides. Turn off the heat, cover again and set aside while you cook the mussels.

Put a large pot over a medium heat. Add the butter or olive oil and shallot with a pinch of salt and cook until soft, about 1 minute.

Turn the heat up to high and add the mussels, samphire and white wine. Put a lid or a plate on top. Give the pan a good shake, then leave to steam for 2 minutes. Stir gently after, making sure all the mussels have enough room to open up. Put the lid back on to cook for another minute. Discard any mussels that remain closed. Divide into two bowls, and serve up with the sliced fried garlic bread. Season to taste and enjoy.

Chef's Tip

There's not much to de-bearding mussels: simply tug upwards on the threads hanging from the shells until they come away, and discard.

Puy lentil and tomato salad with buffalo mozzarella

Cooked lentils seasoned with a good-quality vinegar and olive oil make a fantastic base for a fish or meat main course or for a large salad like this one. Puy lentils are the black freckled variety widely available from supermarkets and health food shops and they have a subtle peppery flavour. They are high in protein, quick to cook and delicious.

Serves 2 as a large salad or 4 as a starter

250g/9oz dried Puy lentils, rinsed and drained
3 ripe tomatoes, roughly chopped
¼ banana shallot or red onion, finely diced
1 garlic clove, finely minced with a pinch of salt
1 celery stick, finely chopped
3 tbsp olive oil, plus extra to serve
3 tbsp sherry, red wine or balsamic vinegar
a small handful of soft herbs, such as parsley, chives or basil (or a mixture), roughly chopped (optional)
salt, flaked salt and freshly ground black pepper
2 buffalo mozzarella, drained and left whole, sliced or broken into chunks (see Chef's Tip)

Add the lentils and 750ml/26fl oz of cold water to a saucepan. Bring to the boil, then reduce the heat to a simmer, cover and cook for 15 minutes, stirring once or twice. Turn off the heat and leave the lid on to rest for at least 5 minutes, by which time the water should have been absorbed.

For the salad, combine the cooked lentils in the same pot or a mixing bowl with the rest of the ingredients, except the mozzarella. Season to taste with salt and pepper.

This lentil salad is best served warm or at room temperature (see Chef's Tip).

To plate up, divide the salad between two plates and top each portion with a mozzarella (whole, sliced or broken into chunks), then season with more pepper, some flaked salt and a drizzle of olive oil.

Chef's Tip

Feta works well as an alternative to mozzarella, if you prefer. Simply sub the mozzarella with 200g/7oz feta cheese, diced or sliced.

This lentil salad can be made up to a day in advance. Make as above, cool, then store in an airtight container or covered bowl in the refrigerator. The next day, allow it to come to room temperature before serving.

Miso butter cabbage conchiglioni with chilli and lemon

My Italian friends can be a little purist about their pasta – it comes from a place of pride, and rightly so, given their regional traditions and considerable respect for the quality of their produce. This dish uses the technique of a classic, simple pasta dish with an olive oil and pasta water emulsion sauce and calls for a little miso paste to give it an umami kick. Use olive oil instead of butter for a plant-based version.

Serves 4

2 tsp salt
2 tbsp olive oil, plus an extra splash
1 head of green cabbage (any variety), about 500g/1lb 2oz, core removed
4 garlic cloves, thinly sliced
1 tsp chilli flakes or 2 fresh red chillies, finely chopped
500g/1lb 2oz dried conchiglioni shell pasta or other dried pasta
2 tbsp white miso paste
2 tbsp butter (or olive oil for a plant-based version)
grated zest and juice of 1 lemon
salt and freshly ground black pepper
freshly grated Parmesan cheese or nutritional yeast, to finish (optional)

Start by putting a large pot of water on to boil, adding the measured salt and the splash of olive oil. Chop your cabbage into equal-sized squarish pieces, each about 5cm/2 inches and set aside.

Fry the garlic with the 2 tablespoons of olive oil and a pinch of salt in a large, non-stick frying pan over a medium-high heat for 1 minute, then add the chilli flakes or chopped chillies, stirring to combine with the garlic.

Next, add in the cabbage and another pinch of salt, then reduce the heat to low while you start cooking your pasta. Cook your pasta in the pot of salted boiling water according to the packet instructions, until al dente.

After the pasta has been cooking for about 5 minutes, transfer about 150ml/5fl oz of the boiling pasta water from the pot to a small bowl or jug and mix with the miso paste and butter (or olive oil) using a fork or whisk. Add this to the cabbage, stir to combine and cook over a low heat for 2 minutes, then turn off the heat and wait for the pasta to finish cooking.

Once cooked, drain the pasta, reserving another 50ml/2fl oz or so of the pasta water. Add the pasta and reserved cooking water to the cabbage mixture and combine well. Season to taste with salt and pepper and the lemon zest and juice, then finish with some Parmesan or nutritional yeast sprinkled on top, if you like.

SBST soup

Spicy, brothy, sour tomato soup. This method is based on a Tom Yum soup recipe I picked up while travelling in Thailand and Cambodia. It's a great comfort dish and a demonstration in how to really impart flavour into a broth.

Serves 2

For the broth

2 tbsp tamarind paste
1 tsp chilli flakes, or 1 fresh red chilli, roughly chopped
3 garlic cloves, skin on, crushed
2 thumb-sized pieces of fresh ginger, skin on, roughly chopped
1 banana shallot, roughly chopped
2 lemon grass stalks, roots removed, each stem cut into three and bruised with the back of a large knife
a big pinch of salt
1 tbsp neutral, olive or coconut oil
250g/9oz fresh raw prawns, heads removed and set aside, peeled (all optional)

For the seasoning

3 tbsp fish sauce, or juice of 1 lime and a little salt
1 tsp chilli powder or hot chilli sauce
1 tbsp tamarind paste
2 tbsp soy sauce
juice of 1 lime

For the rest

200g/7oz dried noodles of your choice
2 plum tomatoes, quartered
raw peeled prawns (saved from the broth ingredients, if using)
1 pak choi or a small handful of other greens, such as spinach, chard or kale, chopped (optional)
a small handful of coriander, roughly chopped

For the broth, combine the tamarind paste and 1 litre/ 1¾ pints of water in a jug or bowl and set aside.

Add all the remaining broth ingredients, except the tamarind water and prawns, to a large pot. Fry over a medium-high heat for 5 minutes.

Next, add the tamarind water and prawn heads (if using). Bring to the boil, then reduce the heat, cover with a lid or plate and simmer for 20 minutes.

Strain the broth into another pot or large bowl, discarding all the vegetables and prawn heads (if using). If you don't have a colander or sieve, you can carefully decant the liquid off with the lid or a plate held over the pot.

Mix the seasoning ingredients together in a small bowl, then stir into the strained broth and set aside.

Now cook your choice of noodles according to the packet instructions (see also page 12), then drain and divide between two large bowls.

Meanwhile, put the pan of strained broth back on the stove, add the tomatoes, prawns (if using) and pak choi or greens (if using) and bring back to the boil, then simmer for 1 minute or until the prawns (if using) just turn pink. Pour the broth over the noodles, finish with the chopped coriander and serve.

'The Kitchen' coconut broth with seasonal vegetables

The Kitchen on Orcas Island is one of our favourite restaurants. Co-owners Charles Dalton and Jasmine Townsend serve incredible Pan-Asian Northwest meals that place organic veggies, island-reared meat and locally caught fish centre stage. You clear your own dishes, canteen-style. They compost the paper plates, saving the rest for the local farm. A model sustainable restaurant.

Serves 2

For the broth

1 banana shallot, diced
2 garlic cloves, crushed
a thumb-sized piece of fresh ginger, peeled and grated or chopped
1 fresh green chilli, chopped
10 sprigs of coriander, stalks finely chopped, leaves saved for garnish
1 tbsp coconut oil
2 lemon grass stalks, roughly chopped
8 kaffir lime leaves, torn, or grated zest of 1 lime
1 tomato, chopped
1 x 400g/14oz can coconut milk
juice of 1 lime
1 tbsp fish sauce, or juice of 1 additional lime and a little salt
1 tbsp soy sauce
salt

To serve

300g/10½oz seasonal vegetables of your choice, such as raw cauliflower or broccoli florets, cooked root vegetables or raw leafy greens, roughly chopped
1 tbsp coconut or olive oil
a pinch of salt
250g/9oz dried noodles of your choice (we recommend flat brown rice noodles)

To garnish and finish

2 tbsp pumpkin seeds
1 tbsp soy sauce
1 lime, cut into wedges
Chilli, Garlic and Sesame Oil (see page 130) or hot chilli sauce (optional)

First, prepare the broth by sweating down the shallot, garlic, ginger, chilli and coriander stalks in the coconut oil with a pinch of salt in a pot over a medium heat for 5 minutes. Add the lemon grass, kaffir lime leaves, tomato, coconut milk and 500ml/18fl oz of water, bring to the boil, then reduce the heat, cover and simmer for 45 minutes, stirring occasionally.

While your broth is simmering, for the garnish, dry-fry your pumpkin seeds in a large, dry, non-stick frying pan over a medium heat until they start to pop, about 2–3 minutes. Deglaze with the soy sauce for 30 seconds and then tip into a dish and set aside.

Next, cook your seasonal veggies in the same pan with the coconut or olive oil, pinch of salt and a splash of water with a lid on over a medium-high heat for 1–2 minutes. Set aside and keep warm to serve later. Or, if just using leafy greens, these can be stirred into the broth 2 minutes before serving.

Next, cook your choice of noodles according to the packet instructions (see also page 12), then drain and divide between two bowls.

To finish the broth, discard the lemon grass and lime leaves from the pot (you can strain out all the other bits, too, for a smooth broth, if you prefer) and season with the lime juice, fish sauce or additional lime juice and salt, soy sauce, and salt to taste.

To assemble, pour the hot broth over the noodles. Add the veggies to the bowls, then garnish with the soy toasted seeds, the reserved coriander leaves and a lime wedge, and finish with a drizzle of chilli, garlic and sesame oil or chilli sauce (if using). Enjoy 'kitchen style' with chopsticks and a spoon.

Chef's Tip

For a more substantial dish, add some cooked protein to the broth as well, if you like. Add about 300g/10½ oz raw peeled prawns or skinless salmon fillet to the finished broth, then bring it back to a simmer and cook for 3–5 minutes. Break the cooked salmon into large flakes before serving.

The vegan burger

As a chef, I liked the challenge of making an appealing, super tasty vegan burger recipe that meat eaters will thoroughly enjoy. If you opt for a regular beef or venison burger instead, you can simply copy the burger sauce and toppings given below to make a classic American-style burger.

Makes 4 burgers

For the burgers
4 tbsp olive oil
400g/14oz mushrooms, finely diced
4 garlic cloves, minced
2 tbsp soy sauce
1 tsp smoked paprika
1 x 400g/14oz can black beans, drained
80g/3oz dried breadcrumbs or chickpea (gram) flour
salt and freshly ground black pepper

For the burger sauce
4 tbsp tomato ketchup
6 tbsp mayonnaise (regular or vegan)
1 tbsp mustard (any)
3 tbsp chopped cornichons
¼ red onion, finely diced
a pinch of salt

For the toppings
1 large tomato, sliced
½ red onion, cut into thin rings
1 Little Gem lettuce, leaves finely shredded

To serve
4 slices of regular or vegan cheese (optional)
4 burger buns of your choice, cut in half (brioche buns are traditional, or use vegan buns)

For the burgers, heat 1 tablespoon of the olive oil in a large, non-stick frying pan over a high heat. Add the mushrooms and garlic with a pinch of salt and cook, stirring occasionally, for 5 minutes. Add in the soy sauce and smoked paprika, stir and turn off the heat.

Place the black beans in a medium bowl and mash with a fork. Add the mushroom mixture, breadcrumbs or chickpea flour and 1 tablespoon of the olive oil and mix until fully combined and the mixture holds together. Taste and adjust the seasonings, if needed.

Using your hands, divide the mixture into four and shape each portion into a patty. Place on a plate and rest in the refrigerator for at least 10 minutes.

To cook, heat another 1 tablespoon of olive oil in your frying pan over a high heat and add your patties, or place them directly over a hot grill or BBQ. Reduce the heat to medium if in a pan, cook for about 5 minutes, then flip over, adding the final tablespoon of olive oil, and cook for another 5 minutes. Avoid squishing the burger down while cooking. Once cooked, the burgers should be nicely coloured and heated all the way through.

If using cheese, top each burger with a cheese slice when almost cooked. Turn the heat off and keep warm in the pan.

Meanwhile, combine all the ingredients for the burger sauce in a bowl. Prepare your toppings, seasoning the tomato slices with salt and pepper.

Toast your buns in a separate dry frying pan over a high heat, until lightly toasted on the cut sides only, or toast them over the grill or BBQ.

To assemble, spread your burger sauce on the toasted buns, add your burgers and top with your garnishes. Burger time!

Späetzle with garlic cream sauce

These German-style dumplings are super quick and tasty and served with a simple garlic cream sauce. They are formed from little spoonfuls of batter dropped into boiling water. Traditionally made with eggs, we've made this recipe fully plant-based with measurements for a version using eggs, too. Serve with wilted greens or a side salad for a more substantial meal.

Serves 2

For the späetzle

300g/10½oz '00' flour
a few grates of nutmeg (optional)
1 tsp salt
300ml/10fl oz plant-based milk, or 250ml/9fl oz dairy milk and 1 egg
2 tbsp olive oil

For the cream sauce

2 tbsp olive oil
1 onion, finely diced
5 garlic cloves, finely chopped
1 tbsp white miso paste
1 tbsp plain flour or '00' flour
100ml/3½fl oz white wine
250ml/9fl oz plant-based or dairy milk
salt

To serve

2 tbsp nutritional yeast or freshly grated Parmesan cheese
wilted greens or a side salad (optional)

First, make the späetzle batter by combining the flour, nutmeg (if using) and salt in a bowl, then whisk in the milk (or milk and egg) until smooth. It should be like a thick pancake batter. Leave it to rest in the refrigerator while you prepare your sauce.

Start the sauce by putting the olive oil into a large, non-stick frying pan and sweating down the onion and garlic with a pinch of salt over a medium heat for 5–7 minutes.

Add the miso paste and stir together, then stir in the flour. Deglaze with the white wine, cook for a minute, and then pour in the milk. Stir well, bring back to the boil, then simmer for a few minutes. Turn off the heat and keep warm until you've made the späetzle.

For the späetzle, bring a large pot of water to the boil with a big pinch of salt.

Take your batter and use two spoons to drop bits of the mix into the boiling water, covering the bottom of the pan (you'll need to cook it in a couple or so batches). When the pan is full, set your timer and boil for 2 minutes. Remove with a slotted spoon on to a plate or into a shallow bowl and drizzle with the olive oil to stop it sticking together. Cook the rest of the batter in batches until it's all done. Save a cupful of the cooking water before discarding the rest.

Finish by adding the späetzle into the warm garlic cream sauce and stirring to coat it all over, adding a splash of the reserved cooking water if the sauce is too thick, or simmering to reduce the sauce (before adding the späetzle), if it's too thin.

Divide the mixture between two bowls. Finish with the nutritional yeast or Parmesan and serve with wilted greens or a side salad, if desired.

Marinated venison fillet with fried potatoes and cabbage slaw

Deer are regularly culled throughout the UK and parts of the US, making venison a sustainable alternative to beef. It's also nearly always free-range and a lean source of protein. We always prepare it the same way with a soy, garlic and ginger marinade, then BBQ or pan-fry it. This tenderizes the meat and brings out a natural, earthy flavour.

Serves 4

1 venison fillet, about 600g–1kg total weight, cut into your desired portion size (150–250g/5½–9oz per person is typical), then tenderized by bashing with a rolling pin, wine bottle or heavy object

For the marinade

2 tbsp soy sauce
2 garlic cloves, chopped
a thumb-sized piece of fresh ginger, peeled and diced or grated
1 tbsp soft light or dark brown sugar, honey or maple syrup
1 tsp vinegar (any type)
1 tbsp neutral or olive oil

For the slaw

¼ red cabbage, finely sliced (use a mandoline, if you have one)
½ red onion, finely sliced
2 carrots, washed and grated
2 tbsp natural yogurt or mayonnaise
grated zest and juice of 1 lime
1 tsp salt
50g/1¾oz chopped raw nuts (pecans are good)

For the fried potatoes

500g/1lb 2oz new potatoes
2 tbsp olive oil

Put all the marinade ingredients into a food bag or suitable dish and mix, then add the tenderized venison portions and mix well. Seal the bag or cover the container and leave to marinate in the refrigerator overnight or for at least an hour at room temperature.

Meanwhile, combine all your prepped slaw vegetables in a large mixing bowl or pot, then add the yogurt or mayo, lime zest and juice, salt and nuts, stirring everything together until evenly coated. Set aside at room temperature until everything else is ready.

For the fried potatoes, follow the recipe on page 13. Once fried and ready, transfer the potatoes to a bowl or plate and keep warm. Use the same frying pan with the leftover oil in to cook the venison (if cooking on a stove).

Bring the marinated venison back to room temperature before cooking, if necessary. Heat up your BBQ (for stove-cooking, see opposite). Carefully put the venison on the grill over the hot coals, cooking it for about 1–2 minutes on each side for medium-rare, until it is nicely charred, or cook for a little longer to your preference. Remove from the grill to rest for 2 minutes. You can baste your meat with the marinade during cooking, if you like, or alternatively, heat it up in a small pan until hot.

If cooking your venison on the stove, put your frying pan over a high heat until it starts to smoke, then add the venison and marinade to the pan and cook and rest as above.

Divide the slaw between the plates and slice the venison into thin pieces. Lay the sliced venison on top of the slaw, add your fried potatoes and drizzle over the combined pan and cooked marinade juices for the final flourish.

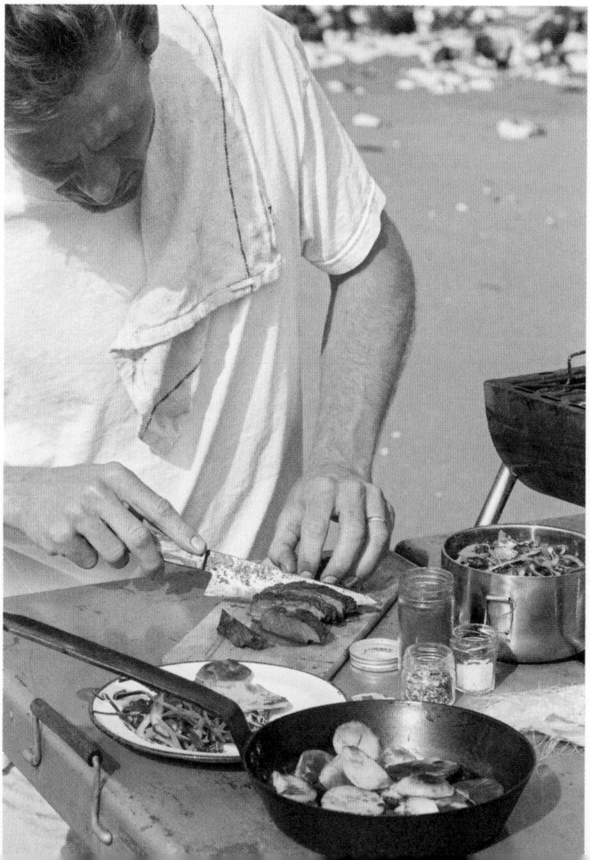

DESSERT

BBQ pear with maple syrup and ice cream

Pears are in season from early Autumn to late Spring. This method works particularly well if your pears aren't quite ripe yet, as the cooking will soften them up a little. If cooking on the BBQ, make sure your grill is clean and the embers are just smouldering. You can cook these in a frying pan or a griddle pan, too.

Serves 2

1 large pear (about 150g/5½oz)
50g/1¾oz walnuts
2 tbsp maple syrup or honey
150g/5½oz vanilla ice cream or Greek-style yogurt (dairy or plant-based)

Simply cut the pear in half lengthways and remove the core. Place the halves, cut-side down, on your hot BBQ or in your preheated dry, smoking-hot griddle or large, non-stick frying pan and cook over a high heat for 5–7 minutes until nicely coloured. Carefully turn over and cook for another couple of minutes to get some marks on the skin-side.

While the pear halves are cooking, toast the walnuts in a separate small pan over a medium heat for about 2–3 minutes until a little coloured, then remove from the heat and set aside.

To serve, place a pear half in each bowl, drizzle with the maple syrup or honey and scatter the toasted walnuts over the top.

Enjoy with scoops of vanilla ice cream or dollops of Greek-style yogurt.

Chilled rice pudding with wild blackberries

You can use arborio or Spanish bomba rice if you can't find the pudding variety. I was a bit late to the rice pudding game but absolutely love it now as a cold, subtly sweet end to a meal. Something about poorly prepared school dinners in the UK probably has a lot to do with its bad rep, but this method will hopefully change your mind. Forage the blackberries in the early autumn or serve with any fruit compote.

A further note: you can flavour the pudding with vanilla extract as is traditional, leave plain or use an edible wild herb or flower such as meadowsweet, elderflower, lavender or thyme. Infuse the herb with the cream and milk by bringing it to the boil, then turning off the heat, letting it sit for an hour, before straining and cooking the rice as below.

Serves 4

250ml/9fl oz milk (dairy or plant-based)
250ml/9fl oz double cream (dairy or plant-based)
100g/3½ oz pudding, arborio or bomba rice
2 tbsp caster or soft light brown sugar or alternative sweetener such as honey or agave syrup
½ tsp vanilla extract (optional)
50g/1¾ oz fresh blackberries or cold cooked/stewed fruit compote of your choice (such as apple, pear or plum)

For the custard (optional)
1 egg yolk
1 tbsp caster sugar
3 tbsp double cream (dairy or plant-based)
or
4 tbsp milk or double cream (each dairy or plant-based)

Put the milk, cream, rice, sugar or sweetener and vanilla extract (if using) in a small pot. Bring to the boil, then reduce the heat and simmer for about 20 minutes, stirring once or twice to break up the rice.

Meanwhile, make your custard (if using) by whisking the egg yolk with the sugar in a mixing bowl. Use your simmering pot of rice as a bain-marie by resting your bowl on top and continue to whisk for about 3–5 minutes until the egg/sugar mixture has thickened and doubled in size (be careful not to get it too hot, otherwise the egg will scramble). Next, whisk in the cream until combined, then continue heating and whisking until the mixture thickens again. Remove from the heat and set aside to add to the rice mixture later.

Once the rice is very soft, turn off the heat and set aside to cool down. Once cooled slightly, you can mix in the egg custard and transfer to a container, then cool and chill in the refrigerator overnight. If not using custard, simply stir the extra 4 tablespoons of milk or cream into the warm rice pudding to loosen, then chill in the refrigerator overnight (see Chef's Tip).

Spoon the chilled rice pudding into small bowls, then serve with the blackberries or fruit compote on top.

Chef's Tip *The chilled pudding will keep, covered, in the refrigerator for up to 3 days.*

Cranachan

Cranachan is a Scottish dessert featuring raspberries folded through whipped cream, with honey, toasted oats and whisky. What a winning combination. Traditionally, it was made during the raspberry harvest in the summer, which gives it a nice celebratory feel. I also like it because it shows a lighter side to Scottish cuisine. Wild raspberries grow in hedgerows in Scotland in late summer; look out for them (and avoid the midges while picking!).

Serves 4

75g/2¾oz porridge oats
50ml/2fl oz whisky of your choice
350ml/12fl oz double cream
2 tbsp honey, maple syrup or other liquid sweetener
1 x 200g/7oz punnet of fresh raspberries

Find 4 small glasses, ramekins or teacups.

Soak three-quarters of the oats in the whisky, ideally overnight or for at least 1 hour.

Pour your cream into a mixing bowl and whip by hand until soft peaks form. This shouldn't take more than a couple of minutes. Once it's lightly whipped, add the honey or other sweetener and the raspberries (keeping a few back to decorate) and carefully fold in.

Toast the remaining oats in a dry, non-stick frying pan over a high heat until a little coloured, about 1–2 minutes, then leave to cool.

To assemble, put half the whisky-soaked oats in the glasses or dishes first, dividing them evenly, then layer some of the raspberry/cream mixture on top, then the rest of the whisky-soaked oats, and the remaining raspberry/cream mixture. Top with the toasted oats and the reserved raspberries, then serve.

Chef's Tip *The cranachan will keep, covered, in the refrigerator for up to 2 days.*

Figs in a blanket

In Greek mythology, figs are associated with Dionysus, the god of wine and hedonism. This may be why they work so well with a number of dessert wines and liqueurs. Our favourite here is Amaretto. You'll need two large pieces of foil for this recipe.

Serves 2

8 amaretti, almond or other soft biscuits, plus extra to serve
4 ripe figs, cut in half
2 tbsp honey, date syrup or other liquid sweetener, plus extra to serve
3–4 tbsp red wine, plus an optional 1 tbsp of Cointreau or Amaretto if you have it
6 tbsp Greek-style yogurt or vanilla ice cream (dairy or plant-based)

Start by making one large foil envelope. Lay out a square piece of foil, approximately 45 x 45 cm (18 x 18 inches). Fold in half, and make three tight creases on each side (left and right). Turn over and make three similar tight creases on the bottom. Open the top to form an envelope for your ingredients.

Break up the biscuits into the foil envelope and put the fig halves on top, then drizzle over the honey or other sweetener and the alcohol. Fold the top over three times to make a seal. Wrap the envelope with another large piece of foil, for protection against tears while cooking.

Place the envelope on the glowing embers in your BBQ or fire and cook for 6 minutes (refer to page 15 for fire cooking temperatures). You should hear a gentle sizzle throughout the cooking time.

Once everything is sufficiently gooey and heated through, carefully undo the envelope and divide between two bowls. Top with yogurt or ice cream and crumble more biscuits on top.

Dark chocolate pots

You just need one pan and four teacups, short glasses or ramekins for this (or you can use one larger dish, if you prefer). No need to buy the supermarket versions – these cost less per portion and can be made fully plant-based if you're able to find a vegan, raw dark chocolate bar.

Makes 4 pots

240g/8½oz good-quality dark chocolate
1 x 400g/14oz can coconut milk, or 400ml/14fl oz dairy milk
2 tbsp soft light brown sugar or caster sugar
1 tbsp butter (optional)
1 tbsp cacao nibs (optional)

Break up the chocolate into small pieces and put in a mixing bowl.

Next, pour the coconut or dairy milk into a small pan, add the sugar and bring to the boil, stirring. Once the sugar has fully dissolved, pour the hot milk over the chocolate, whisking or stirring with a spoon until the chocolate is fully melted.

Stir in the butter (if using) until combined. This gives the pots a silky gloss and helps them to set.

Divide the chocolate mixture between your teacups, glasses or ramekins or pour into a large dish to share, topped with cacao nibs, if using. Place in the refrigerator or cooler/cool box for a minimum of 1 hour before serving. Once chilled, cover, if not serving straight away.

Chef's Tip *These chocolate pots will keep, covered, in the refrigerator for up to 3 days.*

Easy tiramisu (with a shot from a coffee shop)

This is Danny's favourite dessert. I set out to make a giant 30-person tiramisu for his birthday one year and it went down a treat (possibly due to the added twist of hazelnut liqueur). This is tailored for a small kitchen – all you need is a shallow dish/takeaway container, a whisk, a mixing bowl, a spatula/spoon and a decent container or a few wide-bottomed jam jars/teacups, plus time for it to set. Buy an espresso shot from a café nearby if you don't have the means to make an Americano. Tiramisu literally means 'pick-me-up', so I'd recommend adding in some dessert liqueur of your choice – to be enjoyed alongside or in the finished dish as we did a few years ago.

Serves 6

2 shots of espresso (60ml/4 tbsp), or about 1 tbsp (or according to the packet instructions) coffee granules
200ml/7fl oz boiling water (use 250ml/9fl oz, if using coffee granules)
1 x 250g/9oz tub mascarpone cheese
300ml/10fl oz double cream
4 tbsp caster sugar
4 tbsp Kahlua liqueur, Frangelico liqueur, Marsala or dark rum (optional)
1 x 200g/7oz packet ladyfingers (Savoiardi or sponge fingers) – we used 18 fingers – or 200g/7oz sponge or Madeira cake, cut into strips

To decorate
1 tbsp cacao nibs
1 tsp unsweetened cocoa powder

Mix your espresso or coffee granules with the boiling water and pour into a shallow dish or takeaway container.

Take your mascarpone, double cream and sugar and whisk together in a mixing bowl until smooth and the consistency of thickly whipped cream. If using, whisk in your alcohol, 1 tablespoon at a time, until fully combined.

Take your ladyfingers or sponge/Madeira cake strips and very quickly roll each one in the coffee/liqueur mix for about 2–3 seconds. The key is to avoid sogginess by over-soaking them (if there is any leftover coffee/liqueur mix, either drizzle it over the top layer of soaked ladyfingers/sponge cake in the container, or drink it).

Assemble and layer the dessert in the container of your choice (we use our sandwich box, which is 13 x 20cm/ 5 x 8 inches). You can also make individual portions in 6 wide-bottomed glasses or teacups, if you prefer.

Start with a layer of the soaked ladyfingers/sponge cake and then slather on half of your cream mix. Do one more layer of the soaked ladyfingers/sponge and finish with the remaining cream mix. Decorate with the cacao nibs and sifted cocoa powder, then cover (if there's enough spare space at the top of the dessert to do so) and leave to set in the refrigerator for at least 2 hours or ideally overnight.

Lemon posset

In this classic British dessert, the acids from the citrus bind with the protein in the cream to thicken and set the mixture. Lemon is traditional but you can also try blood orange, lime, tangerine or grapefruit. Just be mindful that the amounts of juice for each option may need to be adjusted – the less acidic, the more you'll need to use.

Makes 2 large or 4 small possets in teacups, ramekins or small glasses

300ml/10fl oz double cream
30g/1oz caster sugar
grated zest and juice (about 50ml/2fl oz juice) of 1 lemon, or other citrus zest and juice (see intro and Chef's Tip)
shortbread or ginger biscuits, to serve

Bring the cream and sugar to the boil in a saucepan over a lowish heat, stirring to make sure the sugar has dissolved.

Once the cream has just come to the boil, remove from the heat and stir in all of the lemon zest and juice. Immediately pour into your chosen dishes and leave to cool at room temperature. Once cool, cover and refrigerate for at least 2 hours or until fully set.

Don't worry if it's a little runny, as there are many variables as to how much it sets, particularly if you experiment with the citrus. It will still be a delicious cold, creamy dessert. Serve with your choice of biscuits.

Chef's Tip

If you don't have a grater, thinly peel or cut off a little of the lemon peel (leaving the white pith behind) and finely dice it with a sharp knife.

Wholewheat crêpes with apple compote and cinnamon cream

These light and fluffy wholewheat crêpes work well paired with classic apple and cinnamon flavours. They are super quick to prep and nicely use up apples that have gone a bit soft. For further ease, you can make a large batch of compote in advance and use what you need for this recipe – the leftover compote will keep in an airtight container in the refrigerator for at least 1 week.

Serves 4 (makes 8 crêpes)

For the compote

4 large eating apples or 2 cooking apples (preferably Bramleys)
40–60g/1½–2¼ oz caster sugar
juice of 1 lemon

For the batter

300g/10½ oz plain wholemeal or white flour
2 tbsp caster sugar or other sweetener, such as honey or agave syrup
a pinch of salt
420ml/15fl oz milk (dairy or plant-based)
3 eggs
1 tbsp melted butter, or neutral or olive oil, plus 8 extra tsp for cooking the crêpes

For the cinnamon cream

250ml/9fl oz double cream
1 tbsp caster sugar or other sweetener, such as honey or agave syrup
½ tsp ground cinnamon

First, make the compote. Peel and core the apples, then chop into equal-sized chunks. Add to a saucepan with the sugar (use the 40g/1½oz if using eating apples; use the full quantity if using cooking apples) and lemon juice, then cover and cook down over a medium heat until soft, about 15 minutes. Set aside and leave to cool.

Make your batter by measuring the flour into a mixing bowl. Stir in the sugar and salt, make a well in the middle and whisk in the milk and eggs until smooth, then whisk in the melted butter or oil. Leave to rest for 5 minutes.

To cook the crêpes, heat a teaspoon of melted butter or oil in a large, non-stick frying pan. Once it's hot, add a ladleful or so of the batter, tipping the pan so it thinly covers the base of the pan, then cook over a medium-high heat until nicely browned on both sides, about 1 minute on each side. Remove to a plate and keep warm, while you repeat and cook the rest of the crêpes in the same way to make 8 in total.

To make the cinnamon cream, simply whip the cream with the sugar or sweetener until soft peaks form, then gently fold in the cinnamon.

To assemble, place a generous spoonful of the cold apple compote on each crêpe, roll them up and serve topped with the cinnamon cream.

Flambéed rum bananas with coconut cream

This is based on a famous American dessert from New Orleans called Bananas Foster. Invented in the 1950s, this is a great theatrical dish and is best made in a pan over the campfire. You can also make this in a small kitchen, too, just make sure you pour the alcohol slowly to manage the flames! The rum can be substituted for any dark liquor such as bourbon or whisky.

Serves 2

30g/1oz butter
60g/2¼ oz soft dark brown sugar
2 bananas, peeled and cut in half lengthways
75ml/2½ fl oz rum, bourbon or similar dark liquor
4 scoops of canned coconut cream (see Chef's Tip) or coconut or vanilla ice cream
50g/1¾ oz macadamia nuts or Brazil nuts, roughly chopped (see Chef's Tip)

Take a heavy-based/cast iron (or large, non-stick) frying pan and set it over a grill/rack over an open fire or on your camping stove over a high heat. Melt the butter and sugar together, stirring until fully combined.

Carefully put the bananas in the pan, cut-side down, and continue cooking, letting the sugar/butter mixture caramelize. Turn the bananas over after a couple of minutes.

Carefully pour in your alcohol and stand back to let the flames die down. Continue cooking until everything is nice and syrupy, about 1–2 minutes.

Divide the bananas and boozy caramel sauce between two bowls. Add two scoops of the coconut cream or ice cream to each portion and sprinkle the chopped nuts on top. Enjoy immediately.

Chef's Tip

Keep any leftover coconut cream in an airtight container in the refrigerator for 3–5 days. Use it to top porridge or stir it into a curry.

You can lightly toast the nuts before serving, if you like. Simply toast the whole nuts in a dry, non-stick frying pan over a medium heat for 2–3 minutes, then tip on to a plate, cool and chop.

DRINKS

Rosehip fizz

A simple but refined cocktail suitable for a celebration, and ideal if you have foraged your own rosehips (see page 153) and made your own syrup. Simply add soda water instead of sparkling wine for a tasty, non-alcoholic version.

Serves 1

25ml/5 tsp rosehip syrup (for more info on making your own, see page 153)
about 180ml/6fl oz chilled sparkling white wine of your choice, for topping up

Add the rosehip syrup to a glass and top up with the chilled sparkling wine. Enjoy!

Spiced hot chocolate

Add a little kick to your hot chocolate. Chilli and chocolate is a well-known pairing and hot chocolate with spices added is a popular drink in Mexico.

Serves 2

50g/1¾oz good-quality dark or milk chocolate
2 tbsp unsweetened cocoa powder
¼ tsp cayenne pepper
¼ tsp ground cinnamon
600ml/1 pint milk (dairy or plant-based)
3 tsp white or soft brown sugar or other sweetener, such as honey, agave syrup or date syrup (optional)

Chop the chocolate into little pieces and divide between two mugs.

In a small saucepan, add the cocoa powder, cayenne pepper, cinnamon and a little of the milk, mixing to make a smooth paste, then whisk in the rest of the milk until combined.

Bring to a gentle simmer, stirring occasionally, then stir in your sugar or sweetener (if using).

Pour the hot milk mixture over the chocolate in the mugs, stir well and serve.

Jam jar Cointreau sours

A simple but elegant cocktail, and a good introduction to using egg white, if you've never tried this before.

Serves 2

100ml/3½fl oz (2 double shots) Cointreau
juice of 1 lemon
juice of 1 orange
1 egg white, lightly whisked (just enough to break it down)
ice cubes

Take two clean jam jars and divide the Cointreau, lemon and orange juices and egg white between them.

Add a couple of ice cubes to each jar, leaving a little room spare at the top, cover with the lid and shake it like you mean it.

Unscrew and either enjoy straight from the jar, or strain into two glasses or cups using a tea strainer, discarding the ice before serving.

Hibiscus and ginger tea

We discovered hibiscus from the Jamaican shops in Deptford and Brixton in South London where we live. Jamaicans make an amazing Christmas punch with rum, hibiscus (in the Caribbean, hibiscus flowers are known as 'sorrel'), ginger and lime, but it's also great as a non-caffeinated tea on its own or with ginger. Hibiscus has great health benefits and is packed with vitamin C.

Serves 2

a large thumb-sized piece of fresh ginger, peeled
1 tbsp dried hibiscus flowers
500ml/18fl oz boiling water, to cover

Simply grate the ginger into your teapot, add the dried hibiscus flowers, then pour in your boiling water and leave to steep for about 10 minutes. Strain the tea into your cups or mugs and serve. This tea is equally good served hot or chilled.

Hailee Mary

This is Hailee's winning Bloody Mary recipe. It takes only a little more effort to make your own mix and is so worth it.

Serves 8

a large thumb-sized piece of fresh horseradish, peeled and grated
4 tbsp Worcestershire sauce
2 tbsp hot chilli sauce
grated zest and juice of 1 small lemon
2 tsp celery salt or salt, plus extra to garnish
2 tsp freshly ground black pepper, plus extra to garnish
1 litre/1¾ pints tomato juice
ice cubes
500ml/18fl oz vodka
50ml/2fl oz red wine, ruby port or sherry (optional)
2 limes, each cut into 4 wedges
pickled or sliced fresh vegetables, such as pickled carrot, fennel, celery or cucumber (optional)

In a large serving jug, combine the horseradish, Worcestershire sauce, chilli sauce, lemon zest and juice, celery salt and black pepper. Add the tomato juice and stir well. Cover and refrigerate until chilled, at least 2 hours or ideally overnight.

Pour the tomato juice mixture into eight ice-filled glasses. Add 4 tablespoons (60ml) of vodka into each glass and stir, then top up each glass with a little splash of the red wine, port or sherry. Garnish each drink with an extra pinch of pepper and salt, a lime wedge and some pickled or fresh vegetables (if using).

Kombucha with bourbon

This works as a great whisky/bourbon cocktail. If you make your own kombucha then that would be amazing added to this; otherwise, a good store-bought one will work well – just be sure to use a plain, unflavoured one.

Serves 1

1 tsp honey (optional)
ice cubes
50ml/2fl oz (a double shot) bourbon
250ml/9fl oz kombucha, home-made or store-bought

Spoon the honey over the ice cubes in a jug and stir together until combined. Pour in the bourbon and top up with the kombucha. Pour into a glass to serve.

Michelada

A popular, refreshing Mexican drink, good for low alcohol consumption.

Serves 2

juice of 4 limes
2 tsp hot chilli sauce, such as Tabasco
1 tbsp soy sauce
1 tbsp Worcestershire sauce
2 tbsp tomato juice (or clamato juice)
ice cubes
2 x 330ml/11½fl oz bottles of light lager (Modelo is the best)

For the chilli/salt rim
2 tbsp salt
1 tsp cayenne pepper or medium chilli powder

For the chilli/salt rim, mix the salt and cayenne pepper or chilli powder together in a small dish. Rub a little of your lime juice around the rim of two glasses (or you can use the squeezed lime shells to do this) and dip in the chilli/salt mix.

Divide up the chilli sauce, soy sauce, Worcestershire sauce, remaining lime juice and the tomato (or clamato) juice evenly between your glasses. Add a few ice cubes to each and stir. Pour in your beer. Enjoy!

CONDIMENTS *and* SIDES

Mayonnaise /garlic aioli

Home-made mayonnaise is a total winner and all you need to make it is essentially a small bowl (or cup), a whisk, egg yolks and some oil.

Makes about 300ml/10fl oz

2 egg yolks (save your whites for an omelette or a cocktail)
1 tsp mustard, preferably Dijon
250ml/9fl oz olive oil or a mixture of olive oil and a neutral oil (such as vegetable, sunflower or rapeseed oil)
juice of ½ lemon
salt, to taste
1 garlic clove, minced to a paste with a pinch of salt (if making aioli)

This is easier to make with two people. Using a small bowl (or cup) and a whisk, have someone hold your bowl in such a way so you have a free hand. Vigorously whisk the egg yolks and mustard together in the bowl, then, drop by drop, gradually add and whisk in all the oil until it is incorporated and thickens. You will be whisking for a few minutes, so don't rush adding the oil.

Season with the lemon juice and salt to taste, then fold in the garlic, if making aioli.

This mayo will keep in a sealed (clean) jar or airtight tub in the refrigerator for up to 3 days.

Classic vinaigrette

Nice to know the classic, though we mostly dress our leaves on the plate with extra virgin olive oil and a good-quality vinegar to save on washing up. Sometimes we just use olive oil and lemon juice. Pre-made dressings are usually full of sugar and are an unnecessary cost.

Makes 1 small jarful

2 tbsp white wine, cider or red wine vinegar
6 tbsp olive oil
½ shallot, finely diced
1 garlic clove, minced
1 tsp Dijon mustard
salt and freshly ground black pepper

Put all the ingredients in a clean jam jar, adding salt and pepper to taste, and give it a good shake to combine, or whisk together in a small bowl to emulsify.

Store in the jam jar or an airtight tub in the refrigerator for up to 2 weeks. Shake/whisk before use.

Chilli, garlic and sesame oil

A great storecupboard flavoured oil for finishing curries and Asian dishes.

Makes 1 jam jarful (about 350ml/12fl oz)

10 garlic cloves, finely sliced
100ml/3½fl oz neutral oil (such as vegetable, sunflower or rapeseed oil)
200ml/7fl oz sesame oil
3 tbsp chilli flakes

Fry the garlic in the neutral oil in a small pan over a medium heat until golden brown and crispy, about 2 minutes. Don't let it burn.

Once the garlic is ready, remove from the heat, add the sesame oil and chilli flakes and combine.

Pour into a sterilized jam jar, cool, seal and label, then store in the refrigerator for up to 6 months or more. Shake/whisk before use.

Soy and ginger salad dressing

This is probably the best dressing I've ever tasted. It's very balanced.

Makes 1 small jarful

1 small shallot, finely diced
a thumb-sized piece of fresh ginger, peeled and finely chopped or grated
1 garlic clove, minced or grated
100ml/3½fl oz neutral oil (such as vegetable, sunflower or rapeseed oil)
3 tbsp light soy sauce
1½ tbsp rice wine vinegar
1 tbsp tomato ketchup

Place all the ingredients in a clean jam jar with 1 tablespoon of water and shake together, or whisk everything together in a bowl. Store in the jar or an airtight container in the refrigerator for up to 2 weeks. Shake/whisk before use.

Seaweed sprinkle

A tasty Japanese seasoning that you can make yourself for rice or savoury soups and stews.

Makes 1 small jarful

1 tbsp sesame seeds
1 tbsp dried nori or dulse seaweed
1 tsp celery salt
1 tsp chilli flakes
1 tsp smoked paprika

First, toast the sesame seeds. Tip them into a dry, non-stick frying pan and cook over a medium-high heat for about 1 minute until lightly toasted. Tip on to a plate and leave to cool.

Crush, chop or flake the dried seaweed.

Mix the toasted sesame seeds, seaweed, celery salt, chilli flakes and paprika in a small bowl or in an airtight container.

This will keep in a sealed (clean) jar or airtight container at room temperature for up to a year or more.

Pumpkin seed dukkah

A versatile seasoning that will liven up soups, stews, salads or even some hummus.

Makes 1 small jarful

2 tbsp pumpkin seeds
2 tbsp sesame seeds
2 tsp cumin seeds
2 tsp coriander seeds
1 tsp flaked sea salt

Toast the pumpkin seeds in a dry, non-stick frying pan over a medium heat until they start to pop, about 2 minutes. Tip them on to a chopping board and roughly chop. Set aside in a bowl.

Next, toast the rest of the seeds together in the same pan over a medium heat, moving them around constantly until the sesame seeds start to brown (but not burn!) and the spices start to give off their fragrant aroma, about 2 minutes.

Add to the pumpkin seeds with the flaked salt and mix together, then store in a clean jam jar or an airtight tub at room temperature for up to a year or more.

Nam jim sauce

Our favourite sauce/dressing for seafood and as a dipping sauce.

Makes 1 small jarful

For the base
5 small red or green chillies, or a mixture
3 garlic cloves, peeled
a thumb-sized piece of fresh ginger, peeled
5 sprigs of coriander, finely chopped
1 tbsp palm sugar (if unavailable, use soft light brown, caster or granulated sugar)

To finish
2 tbsp fish sauce, or juice of 2 limes and a little salt
juice of 2–3 limes
1 tbsp neutral or olive oil (optional)

For the base, chop the chillies, garlic and ginger into small pieces, then add to a clean jam jar or small bowl with the coriander and sugar and bash together with the end of a rolling pin or the end of a wooden spoon (or use a pestle and mortar if you have one to hand), until broken up, combined and a paste begins to form.

Mix in the fish sauce (or the extra lime juice and salt), the lime juice and the oil, if using.

Store in the jam jar or an airtight tub in the refrigerator for up to 2 weeks. Shake/whisk before use.

Fermented chilli sauce

This is simply lots of fresh chillies chopped up and packed into a jar with a salt-water solution, which is then left to ferment at room temperature until ready. This fiery sauce goes well with cooked eggs, or use it to spice up curries, soups and stir-fries.

Makes 1 jarful

a handful of fresh long red chillies (about 6–8), finely chopped
1 garlic clove, finely chopped
fine salt
a cabbage leaf

Put an empty clean jam jar or airtight tub on your scales and set the weight to zero. Pack the chopped chillies and garlic into the jam jar or tub and cover with cold water, note down this total weight of ingredients (including the water), then multiply this figure by 0.03. Weigh out that much salt and stir it in (or shake it all together once the lid is in place). For example, 500g/1lb 2oz (total weight of ingredients, including water) x 0.03 = 15g/½oz or 1 tablespoon of salt. This is your salt solution that will deter any unwanted bacteria and maintain the correct pH level to aid lacto-fermentation.

Make sure the ingredients aren't above the water level by weighing them down with something organic such as a cabbage leaf, and put the lid on.

Leave it to lacto-ferment (see Chef's Tip) for 2–4 days in a warm place, or 1–2 weeks in a cool place, unscrewing the lid every now and again to let it burp (release pressure from the fermentation).

Once it has turned very soft and a little funky, strain off almost all the liquid and skim off any white mould (which is harmless and is usually kahm yeast). Transfer to a bowl and crush the chilli mixture with the end of a wooden spoon or a rolling pin (or use a pestle and mortar). Or you can blend it to a runny sauce consistency with a stick blender, if you have the means.

Store in a sealed sterilized jam jar in the refrigerator for up to 3 months or so.

Chef's Tip *Lacto-fermentation is a process in which bacteria breaks down sugars in food and forms lactic acid, creating a different depth of flavour and delicious funkiness to your hot sauce.*

Tahini, garlic and lemon dressing

Use this dressing as a dip, stirred through yogurt or to dress a vegetable salad.

Makes 1 small jarful

4 tbsp tahini
2 tbsp olive oil
1 garlic clove, minced to a paste with a pinch of salt
grated zest and juice of 1 lemon

Place 100ml/3½fl oz of cold water and all the ingredients in a clean jam jar and shake together vigorously, or whisk them together in a small bowl until combined.

Store in the sealed jar or an airtight tub in the refrigerator for up to a week. Shake/whisk before use.

Lime and black pepper

This is so simple but so good. I couldn't believe it was simply these two ingredients mixed together when I tried it in Cambodia. A lot of pepper is grown there, the most esteemed is called Kampot pepper. Use this as a dip for BBQ or roasted meat, such as chicken or chargrilled vegetables.

Simply squeeze some fresh lime juice into a small dish or ramekin and stir in some freshly ground black pepper to taste, adding enough so it's almost like a paste. Use as required on the day it's made.

Harissa sauce

I first made this while working at Poco Restaurant in London. It comes from a great chef pal of ours, Tom Hunt, who's dedicated to campaigning for zero waste and a reformed food system. I've simplified the recipe a little for van purposes while still retaining the original characteristics.

Makes about 5 x 300ml/10fl oz jam jars (great as a gift)

1 jar (about 400g/14oz) roasted red peppers in oil, drained and finely chopped (reserve 2 tbsp of the oil)
3 red onions, finely diced
5 fresh red chillies, seeds left in and finely chopped, or 2 tbsp chilli flakes
2 whole bulbs of garlic, cloves peeled and finely chopped
a pinch of salt
1 tbsp smoked paprika
1 tsp ground cumin
2 tbsp cider, white wine or red wine vinegar
2 tbsp soft dark brown sugar
1 x 1 litre/1¾ pint jar tomato passata (preferably), or 1kg/2lb 4oz fresh tomatoes, cores removed, finely chopped or blended

In a large pot, add 2 tablespoons of oil from the jar of peppers (if available), or use olive oil, then sweat off the onions, chillies and garlic with a pinch of salt over a medium heat for about 10–15 minutes, until very soft and a little caramelized, stirring frequently.

Next, add both ground spices and stir together, then add in the vinegar and brown sugar and stir everything together.

Remove from the heat and leave to cool, then stir in the chopped peppers and passata or chopped tomatoes.

Spoon into sterilized jam jars, seal and label. The sauce can be stored in the refrigerator for up to 3 or 4 weeks.

BBQ Little Gem with Russian salad

You can't go wrong with a potato salad, especially as a BBQ side. Think of Russian salad like the opulent cousin to potato salad. This is our version with charred Little Gem lettuces

Serves 4

1kg/2lb 4oz new potatoes
2 eggs
1 carrot, washed and finely diced
50g/1¾oz green beans, finely chopped, or 50g/1¾oz frozen (thawed) or podded fresh peas
4 tbsp cornichons and/or capers, chopped
2 radishes, diced (optional)
½ bunch of dill or parsley, chopped
1 tbsp Dijon mustard
about 100ml/3½fl oz mayonnaise or soured cream (dairy or plant-based)
juice of ½ lemon
1 Little Gem lettuce, quartered, root kept on
salt and freshly ground black pepper

Put the potatoes into a large pot of cold water, then bring to the boil and cook until tender, adding the eggs to the same pan and cooking them for 6½ minutes for soft-boiled eggs. Once cooked, remove the potatoes to a plate with a slotted spoon, then set aside to cool (they'll be easier to cut once cold). Remove the eggs with the slotted spoon, keeping the hot water for the next step, and plunge the eggs into cold water to cool, then drain, peel and chop.

Put your hot water back on to boil (top it up, if necessary). Add the carrot and cook for 1 minute, then add your green beans or peas and cook for 30 seconds. Drain and set aside.

Next, dice the potatoes and add to a mixing bowl with the cornichons/capers, radishes and herbs, the chopped eggs and blanched vegetables. Add the mustard, mayo or soured cream and lemon juice and mix just enough to bind it all together. Season to taste with salt and pepper and set aside.

Quickly char the quartered Little Gem, cut-side down, over a hot BBQ, or in a hot, dry griddle pan or large, non-stick frying pan over a high heat for 1½ minutes or until nicely charred.

To serve, spread out the leaves of the charred Little Gem quarters and make a mound of the potato salad on top.

Corn on the cob with chilli butter

Corn is harvested in the UK from September to November and is becoming a more popular home-grown crop. Corn on the cob is very straightforward to prepare and is a great addition for late summer BBQs. You could make any flavoured butter or just leave it plain, but we like it with a kick of chilli.

Serves 4

75g/2¾oz butter
1 tsp chilli flakes
1 tsp smoked paprika
a pinch of salt
4 corn on the cob, in their husks

Soften the butter in a jar or small bowl set over a pan of hot water (or at room temperature, if it's warm enough); don't let it melt.

Fold in the chilli flakes and smoked paprika until fully combined, add a pinch of salt and set aside in a ramekin. You could make a batch ahead of time and keep it in an airtight tub or wrapped in foil in the refrigerator for up to a month, if you like.

Next, place the corn cobs with their husks directly over a hot BBQ or grill or in a large, dry, non-stick frying pan over a high heat and cook, turning every now and again, for about 15 minutes; the corn steams in the husk and cooks the kernels perfectly. Adjust the timings based on the heat of your BBQ, grill or pan.

Divide the chilli butter into four portions and place on the serving plates ready for the corn. When the cooked cobs are cool enough to handle, peel off the husks, roll the corn in the chilli butter and enjoy.

FORAGER'S GUIDE

The Joys of Foraging

Foraging is about connection to the landscape and our ancestors through shared knowledge. It provides a link to an original narrative of where our food comes from and promotes a deeper understanding and appreciation of the seasons, senses and what we eat.

By stark contrast, our heavily-industrialized food system relies on intensive farming, monocultures and GM crops, leading to declining soil health and a loss of wildlife habitats. Additionally, lab products and fast food have resulted in an obesity health crisis in the pursuit of profit. Many processed foods are cleverly formulated to strike the perfect balance of fats, sugars and carbohydrates – this is widely known in the industry as the 'bliss point'.

Wild food by comparison can seem obscure, challenging and often bitter to our palates. We grew up and live within these commercial food chains, a system that has also supported the pace of human development within our cultures. While it is possible in an extreme example (and given the right skills) to only live off the land, this isn't realistic. However, wild food does give us an important insight into the true origin of our food and a feeling of empowerment over the food choices we make.

Foraging is a fun addition to exploring the countryside, allowing us to gain useful knowledge, and, ultimately, it leads us to something naturally organic and nutritious that could end up as a main ingredient or at the very least a garnish in a finished dish. From picking young leaves, such as Jack-by-the-hedge, wild garlic and dandelions in the spring for a delicious salad, to finding rare fungi, such as chanterelles and porcini in the autumn, there's a whole range of wild food that's delicious, free and just waiting to be discovered.

In this section we list of a few of our favourite foraged wild foods that are easy for beginners to identify, agreeable to most modern palates and readily available. This shouldn't be used as a definitive guide, and remember that it is very important to always thoroughly research, cross reference between sources and, if you can, learn from someone who can offer you their expertise on foraging safely, considerately and responsibly.

There are many experienced foragers around the country who offer courses and walks you can book and join. As well as the key characteristics, knowing the habitat and appearance throughout the different stages of a plant or fungus's life is crucial to confident identification.

And before you start, there are a number of things to keep in mind:

- Be mindful of local laws and regulations.
- Never eat something you aren't 100 per cent sure about; it can be a perilous activity with many lookalike plants and fungi.
- Never uproot a plant, just pick the leaves so it grows back (and don't pick all of them). It's the law, too.
- Avoid plants below a certain height in areas popular with dog walkers. A good way to tell whether a dog has urinated on a plant is from the distinctive yellow burn.
- Avoid collecting from places near farmland that may have recently been sprayed with pesticides or run the risk of farm runoff. Steer clear of urban areas where authorities may have sprayed chemicals to eradicate pernicious weeds, such as Japanese knotweed (which is ironically an edible).
- Always give your wild food a wash before eating, except for flowers, which should be shaken to remove any insects or bugs. Washing will remove their nectar, and therefore their flavour.

The intention with the handful of recipes we include here is to encourage you to gather the foraged ingredients when you are out and about exploring, and then make the recipes at home, with a bit of prep space and limited equipment, or indeed in your van or small home if you have the means to do so.

Wild garlic or ramsons (*Allium ursinum*)

Found in: Western Europe and Eastern North America
Habitat: damp woodland or near streams
Availability: late February to early June
Rarity: common

A member of the onion (allium) family, wild garlic is available from as early as late February, flowering around the end of April, then starting to wilt in early June. The leaves are like long, elliptical blades of vibrant, green grass tapering to a point. Each plant has up to 25, six-petalled flowers occurring in a tight, rounded cluster at the top of a single stalk.

With a strong but mellow smell of garlic, this is a favourite for foragers. It's easy to identify, abundant and highly versatile. Wild garlic can be eaten raw in pestos and dips, added to soups and stews as you would with spinach or leafy greens, or chopped up and added to pasta dough or dumplings. The buds can be salted and used like capers and the flowers added raw to salads.

Wild garlic pesto

This vibrant and punchy pesto is great added to soups and stews as a garnish, stirred into cooked pasta, or simply served as a condiment. You can use any nuts or seeds but we like almonds or cashews.

Serves 2

80g/3oz wild garlic leaves and stems
100g/3½oz raw almonds or cashew nuts, finely chopped
50g/1¾oz freshly grated pecorino or Parmesan cheese (or choose a vegetarian or vegan version)
100ml/3½fl oz olive oil
juice of ½ lemon

Blanch the wild garlic in a pan of boiling water for 10 seconds, then drain, plunge into cold water and drain again. Chop the wild garlic and mix with all the remaining ingredients in a bowl to make your pesto.

Serve immediately, or store in an airtight jar in the refrigerator for up to 3 days. Serve at room temperature.

Garlic mustard or Jack-by-the-hedge (*Alliaria petiolata*)

Found in: most of Europe, India and Africa; considered an invasive plant in North America
Habitat: waysides, hedgerows (hence the name) and shaded riverbanks or open fields
Availability: a biennial, available in the spring and again in the autumn if the conditions are right
Rarity: common

A welcome sight in the spring, often abundant and easy to identify with its vivid green, slightly toothed soft leaves. You should only pick a few leaves from each plant and avoid older/larger specimens, which can taste too bitter. When ripped or chopped, the leaves give off a distinctive garlic smell.

The flowers are small and brilliant white with four petals and can be added to salads as well as the leaves. You can also blend or chop garlic mustard leaves into sauces and dips or wilt them in soups and stews.

Wood sorrel (*Oxalis acetosella*)

Found in: Europe and North America
Habitat: deciduous and coniferous forests in mossy areas
Availability: March to June
Rarity: common

Similar in size and appearance to the traditional clover, with three folded leaves but brighter green and almost shiny, the five-petalled white flowers have a pretty pink vein and stay closed unless in good sunlight. The signature characteristic is their sharp lemony tang, especially in the leaves. Wood sorrel makes for a great garnish, particularly with fish or in salads.

Please note: both the leaves and flowers can be consumed but only in small quantities, as they contain oxalic acid which is a strong diuretic.

Elderflowers and elderberries (*Sambucus nigra*)

Found in: Europe (except Northern Scandinavia) and North America
Habitat: hedgerows, edges of woodland and urban areas close to train lines and buildings
Availability: flowers in June and July, berries in August and September
Rarity: common

A classic, well-known favourite for its abundant, heady floral flowers in early summer, and the juicy dark berries that appear for a shorter time in late summer/early autumn. It has many varied uses from sparkling wine to elderberry reduction to skincare products.

Elders are commonly found as a small scraggly shrub but can also grow to be more substantial trees with a cork-like bark. Always try to pick the flower heads in the early morning before the sun shines on them to capture the best scent and flavour.

The dark green, slightly toothed leaves are in opposite pairs, arranged in groups of five or seven. The flowers are numerous, comprising tiny white petals with yellowish tops (anthers) arranged abundantly in large, flat-topped clusters up to 25cm/10 inches wide.

The small, reddish to deep purple berries form clusters and are ripe for picking when the clusters turn upside-down. Gather them whole by cutting from the stem, then wash well and strip the berries from the stalks with a fork. Two classic recipes follow below.

Elderflower cordial

Serve this delicious cordial diluted to taste with still or sparkling water (or sparkling white wine) or add it to a gin and tonic. Alternatively, try using it to flavour desserts, such as the French Toast recipe on page 28, or to sweeten dishes such as pancakes or porridge.

Makes about 2 x 750ml/26fl oz bottles

1 litre/1¾ pints boiling water (from the kettle)
1.25kg/2lb 12oz caster sugar
grated zest of 1 lemon, whole lemon then sliced
2 tbsp citric acid
15 freshly-picked elderflower heads, shaken to remove insects (not washed)

Pour the boiling water into a mixing bowl and stir in the sugar until dissolved.

Stir in the lemon zest and slices of lemon and the citric acid, then add the whole flower heads. Cover and leave to sit at room temperature for 24 hours.

Once it's ready, strain through a clean tea towel, a fine mesh strainer or preferably some muslin cloth. Pour into sterilized, airtight bottles or containers, seal, label and store, unopened, in the refrigerator for up to 6 months. Once opened, store in the refrigerator for up to 1 month. Use as required (see intro).

Elderberry vinegar

This is a delicious vinegar to use in dressings for root vegetable salads, such as beetroot, or stirred into winter stews. Please note: this needs 1–2 months to mature before use.

Makes about 500ml/18fl oz

10 freshly-picked elderberry heads full of ripe berry clusters, washed
500ml/18fl oz red wine vinegar, or 300ml/10fl oz red wine vinegar and 200ml/7fl oz red wine
75g/2¾ oz caster sugar

Using a fork, strip the berries from the stalks and place in a non-metallic bowl or container (we use a glass/Kilner jar or plastic container) along with the vinegar or vinegar and red wine mix, then cover tightly and leave to infuse in a cool, dark place for 1–2 months.

After this time, strain the liquid into a saucepan, stir in the sugar, then bring slowly to the boil and simmer for 1 minute to dissolve the sugar. Pour into a sterilized bottle or jar, seal, label and store in a cool, dark place (or the refrigerator) for up to a year or longer. Once opened, it keeps well, too.

Marsh samphire (*Salicornia europaea*)

Found in: European and North American coastlines
Habitat: rocky beaches, salt marshes and mudflats
Availability: early summer (May onwards)
Rarity: uncommon, though abundant where it grows

A popular ingredient with chefs and often served with seafood, this briny succulent is a member of the goosefoot family and is similar to green beans or asparagus when washed and quickly blanched. There are several varieties but they are difficult to distinguish from one another and all are edible. It's an annual, appearing in early summer and turning reddish towards the end of its season.

Samphire vinegar

Infused with samphire, this vinegar makes an interesting addition to your storecupboard. It can be used to dress salads or flavour mayonnaise, or served with seafood or other savoury dishes. Please note: this needs 2–3 months to mature before use.

Makes about 500ml/18fl oz

50g/1¾oz fresh samphire
6 dried allspice berries
1 shallot, diced
500ml/18fl oz rice wine vinegar or cider vinegar

Place all the ingredients in a clean jar or bottle, cover tightly and leave in a cool, dark place for 2–3 months.

After this time, strain into a sterilized bottle or jar, seal, label and store in a cool, dark place (or the refrigerator) for up to a year or longer. Once opened, it keeps well, too.

Meadowsweet (*Filipendula ulmaria*)

Found in: throughout Europe and North America
Habitat: damp meadows, marshes, swamps, and commonly found next to rivers
Availability: flowers June to September
Rarity: uncommon, but grows together or in large patches

Meadowsweet is easy to recognize with its fluffy, candy floss-like flower heads, often growing in big swathes in damp fields along riverbanks, reaching up to between 1–2 metres/3–6 feet in the air. The flower heads smell and taste like honey and almonds and can be dried and used to flavour beer or wine, to drink as tea or be made into a cordial similar to elderflower cordial.

Meadowsweet cordial

2 litres/3½ pints water
500g/1lb 2oz sugar
juice of 2 lemons
1 large bunch Meadowsweet flowers (about 50 heads)

Bring the water to the boil and add half the sugar and the lemon juice. Add the flowers into the pot, then bring back to the boil and simmer for 2 minutes. Turn off the heat and leave to infuse overnight.

The next day, strain the flowers from the liquid, add the remaining sugar and bring to the boil for 5 minutes. Decant into sterilized jars and use in cocktails, or as a cordial.

Rosehips or dog rose (*Rosa canina*)

Found in: throughout Europe and North America (except the far north)
Habitat: hedgerows, wasteland and woodland margins
Availability: August to November
Rarity: common

Rosehips come from the wild rose or dog rose, a common, thorny plant that produces light pink flowers in early summer and bright red oval fruits later in the year. The hips are actually a swelling part of the stem, which contains the hairy fruits and seeds within. They are best picked just after the first autumn frost when they will be at their ripest and most flavourful.

A favourite in our wild food calendar for its extremely high concentration of vitamin C, with a flavour reminiscent of rhubarb and custard, we make enough rosehip syrup every year to see us through the winter. We use an old recipe from the Ministry of Food from 1943 to make our rosehip syrup. It can be used as a flavouring for milk puddings, ice cream or almost any dessert, or simply diluted with water or sparkling wine as a refreshing drink.

Horseradish (*Armoracia rusticana*)

Found in: Europe and North America; native to Western Asia
Habitat: roadsides, wasteland and field margins
Availability: flowers May to September
Rarity: uncommon

Once you have your eye dialled in to horseradish, it's hard to miss. If you are familiar with dock leaves (used to nurse nettle stings), horseradish is similar looking but has longer, taller straight stems and slightly toothed and waxy leaves without the red spots found on dock leaves.

As horseradish is a root, you will need the landowner's permission to dig it up. With a large and sprawling root system, too, you'll need a spade.

To make a fresh horseradish sauce, clean it thoroughly, then peel and grate the fresh root into a bowl, mix with crème fraîche or soured cream, and season with salt.

Sloes/sloe berries/blackthorn (*Prunus spinosa*)

Found in: mainland Britain and naturalized in North East America
Habitat: hedgerows and woodland margins
Availability: early Autumn to December
Rarity: uncommon, though widespread and native to the UK

Also known as blackthorn, these very tart berries are the ancestor of cultivated plums. They grow on a stiff, dense shrub with alternate, oval-shaped dark green leaves, very sharp thorns (the same ones used to make the infamous crown) and flowering white petals with bright orange anthers in April. The berries are green at first, then ripen to dark blue/black. They are too acidic to eat straight from the tree, but can be turned into a good jelly, or the famous sloe gin (see below) – which is highly recommended.

As with rosehips, ripe sloes are best picked just after the first frost (the blistered skins will combine with the alcohol more harmoniously). Alternatively, make a small slit in each unfrosted berry with a sharp knife, or put them in the freezer overnight to create the same effect.

Sloe gin

This is an excellent winter tipple, served chilled or at room temperature in a shot glass. Sloe gin can even be used as a boozy cordial in desserts; for example, folded through whipped cream or added to crumbles/pies or jelly. Please note: this needs a couple of months or so to infuse before use.

Makes about 750ml/26fl oz

250g/9oz ripe sloes (see general info above for the ideal time to pick)
125g/4½oz caster sugar
750ml/26fl oz gin (or you can use vodka or brandy)

Mix the sloes with the caster sugar and fill a large, wide-bottomed jar or several jars with this mixture, then top up with the gin (or vodka or brandy). Cover tightly, label and store in a cool, dark place for a couple of months or so, shaking the jar(s) occasionally. The sloe gin (vodka or brandy) will be ready just in time for Christmas (convenient).

Strain into a sterilized bottle, seal and label. Serve chilled or at room temperature (see intro). Try the gin-soaked berries, too, and eat as they are, as they will have lost their bitter edge and soaked up the gin flavour (but be careful of the stones!).

Sweet chestnuts (*Castanea sativa*)

Found in: Europe and North America
Habitat: woodland and parks
Availability: September to November
Rarity: common

A tall, deciduous tree with single, serrated, spear-shaped leaves and whitish-yellow catkins, that flowers late in the summer. The green prickly fruit falls in the autumn and reveals two or three shiny nuts.

The best chestnut trees are the very large, old ones, which will shed their fruit early in the autumn. Gloves are a good idea to pick the nuts from the spiky husks, or some skilful footwork.

Fresh, sweet chestnuts must always be cooked before eating (either roasted or boiled), then peeled.

Chanterelle mushrooms (*Cantharellus cibarius*)

Found in: Europe and North America
Habitat: mostly broadleaved woods/forests, particularly around beech trees, but also found in pine forests
Availability: July to October
Rarity: rare

These are widely considered one of the most desirable mushrooms, and to a forager, stumbling upon chanterelles is like striking gold. They are egg-yolk in colour with paler flesh when cut and a pleasant aroma of apricots. The gills are forked, shallow and continuous with the stem. The cap is funnel-shaped with irregular lobed and curly margins. Classically, chanterelles are fried in butter and served on toast with scrambled eggs.

Please note: there are some lookalikes that can cause severe stomach upsets, including the aptly named false chanterelle.

Index

US/UK glossary

aubergine/eggplant
autumn/fall
beetroot/beet
biscuits/cookies
black pudding/blood sausage
broad beans/fava beans
caster sugar/superfine sugar
celery stick/celery stalk
chard/Swiss chard
chickpeas/chickpeas or garbanzo beans
chilli/chile (fresh or dried)
chilli flakes/chile flakes (or red pepper flakes)
chilli powder/chili powder
chilli sauce/chili sauce
chopping board/cutting board
cooking apple/baking apple
coriander/cilantro (fresh)
courgette/zucchini
crisps/potato chips
double cream/heavy cream
frying pan/skillet
greaseproof paper/wax paper
griddle pan/grill pan
grill/broil
grill/broiler
jug/pitcher
kitchen cloth/dish towel or kitchen towel
kitchen paper/paper towels
knob of butter/pat of butter
Little Gem lettuce/Boston lettuce
Madeira cake/pound cake
mature cheese/sharp cheese
mince(d)/ground
muslin/cheesecloth
natural yogurt/plain yogurt
non-stick/nonstick
omelette/omelet
packet/package
parcel/pocket or parcel
pak choi/bok choy
passata/strained tomatoes
pepper (red, green, yellow)/bell pepper
pitta bread/pita
plain flour/all-purpose flour
porridge oats/rolled oats
porridge/oatmeal porridge/oatmeal [finished dish]
prawns/shrimp
punnet/carton or container
Puy lentils/French lentils
rapeseed oil/canola oil
rocket/arugula
sieve/strainer
single cream/light cream
soured cream/sour cream
spring greens/collard greens
spring onions/scallions
starter/appetizer or starter
stoned/pitted
storecupboard/pantry
sweetcorn/corn
tea towel/dish towel
tomato purée/tomato paste
whisky/whiskey
wholemeal/whole wheat

Acknowledgements

We are very grateful to Lucy and all at Pavilion Books for commissioning this creative project, taking a chance with us as first time authors and reminding us that opportunities can come about in surprising ways.

To all our friends and family in the UK and USA for the encouragement and positivity throughout this process. We couldn't have made this book without your ideas, contributions, and taste testing along the way.

To Cara, our editor who guided us throughout the journey of writing this book. For Nicky our designer, who found the best locations in Kent and Sussex and went above and beyond with the design and art direction. For Holly, who brought such a considered, joyful style to this book with her photography. Becks, Rachael and Joanna, thank you for styling each dish so beautifully and authentically. Everyone's energy, collaborative spirit and excellent company made each of our shoot days so memorable this summer. Also thanks to Sam at Hook Farm and Virginia at Broadstairs location house.

Danny would like to thank all the chefs he has worked with over the years who provided an invaluable, supportive community and who also inspired many of the recipes in this book - in particular, Jamie Ross, George Livesey and Tom Hunt.

And finally, to all who bring a sense of adventure and a resourceful outlook on their travels, as well as an appreciation and respect for the natural world.